2021

Th

F

The Pathway to Peace, Joy, and Happiness
Where Miracles Become Expectations

Jon Lovgren

Because of the dynamic nature of the internet, any web addresses or links contained in this book may have changed since publication and may no longer be valid. The views expressed in this work are solely those of the author and do not necessarily reflect the views of the publisher, and the publisher hereby disclaims any responsibility for them.

The author of this book does not dispense medical advice or prescribe the use of any technique as a form of treatment for physical, emotional, or medical problems, and suggests that you seek the advice of a physician, either directly or indirectly. The intent of the author is only to offer information of a general nature to help you in your quest for emotional, spiritual, and physical well-being. In the event you use any of the information in this book for yourself, which is your constitutional right, the author and the publisher assume no responsibility for your actions.

Any references to historical events, people or places are used fictitiously. Names, characters, and places are products of the author's imagination.

ISBN: 978-1-64606-826-5 (paperback)
Library of Congress Control Number: 1-7441001681

Front cover image by: Rob Williams ~ Designer ~
Fiverr.com/cal5086
Book design by: Jon Lovgren
Editing by: Jennifer Jas ~ Words With Jas
Proofing by: Laurie Teitelbaum

First printing: May 2019
Hawaiian Stickbug Productions
77-6425 Kuakini Hwy, C2-21
Kailua Kona, HI 9674-0
www.themagicwords.net
808-365-7666

Dedication

This book is dedicated to:
Madame Pele'
Mahalo nui loa for your Wisdom teachings ...

And

The Kingdom of Hawai'i
May we show the rest of the world aloha.

Zachary Bradford Gibson
"The Kava Man of Kona"
May 12, 1966 – November 4, 2018

Zak brought kava back to life on the big island and introduced it to the rest of the world. Many of the kava bars on the mainland started as a result of a visit to Kanaka Kava.

Thank you, Zak. You touched so many lives and will always be remembered.

Mahalo nui loa.

Your Kanaka Kava legacy lives on!

EalohaE

Epigraph

Pathway to Peace
Where Miracles Become Expectations

~~ Jon Lovgren

There are two times to forgive:
Now and Later

~~ Kahuna Harry Uhane Jim

Acknowledgments

My sincere thanks and heartfelt gratitude to all of those who pushed my buttons, tripped my triggers, and helped me to see the things that were hidden within that no longer served my higher purpose. For without those experiences, I could not have come to a place of truly understanding what Unconditional Love really means.

To my Father, John C. Lovgren, Sr. We did not speak to one another for over thirty years, and when we reconnected, it was with complete love and forgiveness. It took us thirty years, but we are Pono!

My Father said, *"You know I am a staunch agnostic. I do not buy into any of that spiritual or religious stuff, but this is a good philosophy! It can't hurt, it might help." ~~ John C. Lovgren, Sr.*

To my mentor: Kahuna Harry Uhane Jim
Carissa Marie Lovgren ~ Showed me that anything is possible
Kelly Marie Kukuna Lengel ~ Always in truth
To my ohana (family): Too many to list here…

Laurie Teitelbaum: There are no words in the English language to express the deep gratitude I have for Laurie. This book would not be what it is without her love, her mana, her relentless pursuit of perfection. The best words I can come up with are Hawaiian: Mahalo nui loa and Aloha no au ia oe. I hope I did not wear you out – there are two more books already in process. LoL

Foreword for The Magic Words
by Jacob Teitelbaum MD

Humanity, both individually and collectively, is going through a major period of awakening. In fact, this has already happened. We simply are just starting to wake up to this fact.

As we wake, we are getting glimmers of how broken our institutions are. Medicine. Politics. Education. Economics. Many of us are frustrated over our seeming inability to affect the changes we know are needed.

But as been said, when one cuts out the rotting parts of an institution, good people fall out. Truly, to change these institutions requires changing ourselves.

Doing so easily and quickly is the gift of Ho'oponopono. As you do it, you will find yourself, and then the world around you, changing ever more deeply.

How can this be?

Have you ever noticed that each of us is the star of life's vast movie? Amazing, as over seven billion different movies are going on at once. Yet, this is because by our choices and our actions (or all too often simply reactions), we are both writing and producing the script in each moment. When we feel powerless, we are doing this by reacting unconsciously.

It is by becoming conscious that we reclaim wholeness, and thus our individual power. We do this in several ways. One is by learning to unconditionally love and accept all the parts of ourselves. This requires self-forgiveness and forgiveness of others.

But here is the shocking truth. Forgiving others is mostly about forgiving ourselves. Self-forgiveness for feeling weak and powerless to say no. For being afraid of intimacy. For feeling sexual. For wanting more. Even for beating ourselves up for being in pain.

All of our perceived injuries, and the associated hurts that we carry, in truth come from how these leave us feeling about ourselves. And in forgiving ourselves, we come to be able to love every part of ourselves. Then we realize that there is nothing left about the other person for us to forgive.

THEN, when we have forgiven and lovingly owned all parts of ourselves, we truly step into the power that is wholeness. What others think about us is no longer important. Instead of guiding our lives by trying to please everybody else, we learn to tune in to what feels good to us. Rather than doing what everyone else has told us that we should do to make them happy. In a word, we become authentic.

When we do this, many people find that many untreatable conditions, such as fibromyalgia and chronic pain, start to dissipate. The physical and other cures start to flow naturally and easily into your life.

But how can we learn to forgive ourselves? In fact, how can we even become aware of the deep unconscious forces within us that shape our personal reality? We can try decades of psychotherapy, but this only takes people so far. And usually nowhere near far enough.

Now, ancient Hawaiian tradition offers us a new, simple and remarkably powerful tool. As you simply repeat the four lines which make up Ho'oponopono, you'll find that what underlies your uncomfortable feelings will start coming to the surface in layers. Then, as if by magic, they start resolving and disappearing. It may seem unlikely that this is possible. But it is. You will see as you do it! You'll also start to understand how the sweet and beautiful Aloha spirit came to be.

As you learn and practice Ho'oponopono, you will find yourself moving into self-awareness, self-acceptance, and self-love. Your life will change – dramatically. Along with your relationships. Followed by institutions. And then the world.

It is interesting, but one person lovingly owning their authenticity can be more powerful than millions of people who have not.

Ready to transform your life? And the world? Read on!

Preface

I was first introduced to ho'oponopono at a workshop led by James Arthur Ray in 2007. I started saying it sporadically at first, and sometimes there were weeks between. I began noticing subtle differences in the way I felt and changes in my life. I did not fully understand at the time, but what I did notice was that the more often I said ho'oponopono, the better I felt and the more my life changed.

In 2011, I found myself homeless and jobless. I was going through chronic low-back pain and at the time could not work in an office environment. I was unable to sit for longer than twenty minutes at a time – not an acceptable condition in a corporate office. I remember saying to myself, "I need a job where I can work from home." I began saying ho'oponopono all the time, over and over, and one day, out of the blue, I received an email from a contracting company asking if I was interested in working for a high-tech computer company, and oh by the way, it would be working from home and they would send me a laptop. YES! I am interested!

The hiring process took about two months, and near the end of that period, I can remember lying in my bed thinking, "Ugh, this is taking so long. Did they find something in my background check? Is this really happening or is this one of those 'too good to be true' scenarios?" I very quickly started saying ho'oponopono over and over and I changed my thinking to visualizing/imagining receiving the email with the flight and hotel reservation to go to the company orientation. I visualized myself going to the airport, boarding the plane, the flight to Dallas, the cab ride to the hotel, checking in, and settling into my room. I visualized with as much detail as I could, continuing to repeat ho'oponopono as I was imagining it all happening. Two days later, I received an email with the flight/hotel reservations. I have been in that job ever since – it is my dream job. It is not work; it is something I look forward to every day.

When I received the email with the air/hotel reservations, I knew at that moment that there was something more than meets the eye about ho'oponopono. I began embracing it and embodying it, saying it as often as I could. The miracles continued to happen and soon became expectations. Extremely outstanding or unusual events, things, or accomplishments became everyday occurrences rather than "once in a lifetime" events. Hence the reason I say, "Miracles become expectations."

When we practice ho'oponopono diligently and consistently, it eventually ceases to be a practice and becomes a lifestyle, one of peace, joy, happiness, and love! We live in a place of constant love, humility, compassion, and gratitude, embracing and loving the most difficult of moments and days while understanding that these difficult times are simply showing us what wants to be healed within us. This happens when we realize that we now have conscious communication with our unconscious minds.

Continuing our ho'oponopono lifestyle, we come to know unconditional self-love. We become unshakable. We no longer judge others as we now understand that all judgment is self-judgment. We begin to feel a oneness with all that is. We are now living pono! When we are living pono, truth is easy to stay in, to speak, and to hear. We understand that we are not responsible for anyone else's feelings, only our own.

It is with Aloha (love) that I release this culmination of forty-plus years of searching for answers in ancient texts, mystic practices, quantum physics, and life in general, to come to the simplest, most profound, most effective approach I have had the pleasure to learn and practice.

It is my pule' (prayer) that you embrace this practice as I have until it becomes a lifestyle. It is my belief that if enough people lived pono, we would have world peace!

Introduction

What does it mean to "Live Pono"? It means living a life of being at one with everyone and everything.

The spiritual journey is oftentimes a lonely one. Not lonely in the sense of being alone; but rather, lonely when one is in a relationship but unable to share spiritual experiences in a way the other one understands. We have companionship in that relationship, but at some point, that may no longer be enough to keep the spark alive. And often we reach that point, but continue in the relationship anyway, basically hoping that something will change, but not knowing exactly what needs to change.

After a period of waiting for change, we may come to the point of understanding that nothing else is going to change, so "I must be the change." If I am feeling stifled or not able to express myself fully, I need to change my environment and place myself in one of authenticity and love. To be someplace where I can feel 100-percent comfortable just being who I am in this moment, whatever the moment is. That is what it means to live pono; to just be real. Be you, whoever that is in any given moment. This is not so easy to do, especially from the environments in which many of us grew up.

What does it mean to be "real"? It means to live within your feelings, from your heart, at all times. This is very difficult to do when we are surrounded by, let's just say, our "ego." For example, running around doing our best to become the success we think someone else wants us to be. Most, if not all of us, go through that because that is what we were taught, to "follow in your parents' footsteps," go to school, get good grades, go to college, get a degree, get a good job, stay with it until you retire, build that retirement fund so you can do whatever you want for the rest of your life (if you feel up to it).

Why not do whatever you want for the rest of your life starting now?!

At some point, we have a desire, a passion, a command almost, to just be ourselves, to follow our hearts, and to trust that our hearts will never lie to us. Growing up, we learned to follow certain paths and guidelines as laid out by pretty much anyone older than us at the time. We made agreements with ourselves that it must be so, because they said so. We looked around and we saw everyone else doing the same, and we all learned to connect on that level of understanding. By doing this, we strengthened that very belief system because we reinforced it within one another, losing ourselves in the process.

And then at another point in our lives, usually the early, pre-teen years, something happens and we have questions that cannot be answered, or we present ideas that we feel are true and plausible, yet many of us are reprimanded for having those thoughts or ideas, so we learn to shut that part down and keep them to ourselves. Thus, begins the loneliness that is often associated with some spiritual paths.

Because we learn the "follow in your parents' footsteps" behavior at an early age, it is easily transposed throughout our lives. Those memories live in our unconscious, our muscles, our fascia, and even our very bones. Because these events happened so long ago and had so much reinforcement, they became automatic. They trigger the energy we are exuding that attracts the people into our lives to help us experience and re-live those memories. For many of us, it is like the proverbial "walking on eggshells." We are very careful about what we say and are especially cautious about expressing our feelings about anything of importance, for fear of retribution or judgment.

Something happens to us and for us, when we come into living from our hearts. It is difficult to explain and understand until we experience it. However, I will do my best to explain it for you or for you to explain to a friend or a loved one who says that they are on a spiritual path. Please understand that, in some respects, the path is truly not a choice for us. We come to realize that it is what we came here to do in this physical form. Pretty much all the ancient texts refer to us as spiritual beings having chosen to have a physical experience. That being so, then we, as spirits, have chosen to come into these lives in order to experience life and all of its circumstances.

We all know this at some level, but as we came into this existence, we conveniently forgot why we came here. Therefore, we spend much of our lives doing our best to understand that – to figure out the why. At some point, it all makes sense, but only to ourselves and, of course, others who have walked that path and have come out on the other side.

One cannot truly understand how any given situation feels unless and until one has been through something similar in their own life path. You cannot truly understand what it means to have your house burn down and all that goes with that, unless you have lived through your own house burning. We can imagine what something feels like but cannot truly know it except through experience.

Herein lies the difficulty for someone doing their best to explain how it feels to come into their heart-calling. Knowing that whoever they are explaining their purpose to cannot possibly understand at the same level because they have not yet felt that same calling.

We always have been and always will be; hence, there is no longer any blame. We can no longer blame our parents or anyone else for how our lives are turning out.

We will look into how it works at the deepest levels through an exploration of quantum physics, metaphysics, neuroplasticity, biology, neuroscience, and consciousness.

We will reference a number of other books that help us take ho'oponopono to the deeper levels and understand how to use it to bring ourselves to a place of peace, no matter what is going on around us.

What my father said is worth repeating:

> *"You know I am a staunch agnostic, I do not buy into any of that spiritual or religious stuff, but this is a good philosophy! It can't hurt, it might help."*

And with that, I implore you to keep an open heart and mind as we explore concepts, ideas, and the magic of ho'oponopono.

Table of Contents

Chapter 1 – First Things First
Aloha Spirit
It Is Law

"Aloha Spirit Required Here – If you can't share it today, please visit us some other time. Mahalo"

Where do we begin?

We begin in Hawai'i. To fully understand ho'oponopono, we must first understand Aloha and Aloha Spirit.

Aloha Spirit is Hawai'i state law:

> **§ 5-7.5 "Aloha Spirit"**
> The Aloha Spirit is the coordination of mind and heart within each person. It brings each person to the Self. Each person must think and emote good feelings to others. In the contemplation and presence of the life force, Aloha, the following unuhi laulâ loa (free translation) may be used:
>
> Akahai, meaning kindness, to be expressed with tenderness;
> Lôkahi, meaning unity, to be expressed with harmony;
> Olu'olu, meaning agreeable, to be expressed with pleasantness;
> Ha'aha'a, meaning humility, to be expressed with modesty;

Ahonui, meaning patience, to be expressed with perseverance.

These are traits of character that express the charm, warmth and sincerity of Hawai'i's people. It was the working philosophy of native Hawaiians and was presented as a gift to the people of Hawai'i. Aloha is more than a word of greeting or farewell or a salutation.

Aloha means mutual regard and affection and extends warmth in caring with no obligation in return.

Aloha is the essence of relationships in which each person is important to every other person for collective existence.

Aloha means to hear what is not said, to see what cannot be seen and to know the unknowable.

In exercising their power on behalf of the people and in fulfillment of their responsibilities, obligations and service to the people, the legislature, governor, lieutenant governor, executive officers of each department, the chief justice, associate justices, and judges of the appellate, circuit, and district courts may contemplate and reside with the life force and give consideration to The Aloha Spirit.

[L 1986, c 202, §1]

* Aloha means to hear what is not said, to see what cannot be seen and to know the unknowable.

This is hard to make sense of at first. However, the more we practice ho'oponopono, the more we begin to understand what this truly means. By the end of this book, this will all make sense.

Ancient texts remind us that we are spiritual beings first, having chosen to have a human experience. Yeah, okay, so what? So, what does that mean? We do not all experience everything the same way, hence the challenges of communication – how to describe what we are thinking, imagining, etc.

In the beginning was a void, nothing, no thing, known as ein soph or ein soph aur in Kabbalah. Then there was a light, the beginning of creation, zero-point field, the big bang, and this Universe was born and has been growing exponentially ever since. It is Energy, vibrating at different frequencies. Similar frequencies were attracted to one another and consciousness was born. From consciousness came the desire to have a human experience. The vibration of this thought attracted the vibrations matching that frequency, and spirit created the human form.

The only way to fully understand Aloha, "... to hear what is not said, to see what cannot be seen, and to know the unknowable," is to live in Spirit. Live in Love. Live in the Spirit of Aloha. There is a saying in Hawai'i that has almost disappeared over the years:

e aloha aku (I send aloha)
e aloha mai (I receive aloha)

The only way to get more aloha is to give all we have. Yes, we can give a little, get a little, but we will never get more until we give all we have – then and only then do we receive more.

The more we practice ho'oponopono, the more we live in aloha, the more we understand hearing what is not said, seeing what cannot be seen, and knowing the unknowable. Eventually, Aloha Spirit becomes our lifestyle.

The best way I have found in over forty years of studying and practicing different modalities is a consistent, diligent practice of ho'oponopono. Ho'oponopono treats the cause; everything else I practiced only treated the symptom. It is not until we address the cause that the discomfort is completely healed.

The funny thing is, most of us seem to have to be at the bottom before we do something new to change our situation. We will begin here in the next chapter, working our way up the vortex, the spiral, if you will.

Chapter 2 – Two Times to Forgive
Ho'oponopono
The Pathway to Peace

"When one door of happiness closes, another opens; but often we look so long at the closed door that we do not see the one which has been opened for us."

-Helen Keller

Welcome to Ho'oponopono.

I Love You
I'm Sorry
Please Forgive Me
Thank You

Ho'oponopono is a very powerful, ancient life-transforming meditation that originated in Hawai'i and has a long history of healing the individual and reuniting families. Over the years, the traditional form of ho'oponopono has gradually faded and is only practiced in its original form on rare occasions, and only by a select few kahuna lapa'au (healer); however, in 1976, Morrnah Nalamaku Simeona began the transformation of ho'oponopono into what it is today.

Morrnah is responsible for updating ho'oponopono so that it no longer requires the presence of a practitioner or anyone else, thereby allowing individuals to perform their own healing. Morrnah taught ho'oponopono to small and large groups, hospitals, universities, and even the United Nations personnel. Her prized student during this time was Dr. Ihaleakala Hew Len, a staff psychologist at the Hawai'i State Hospital. Dr. Hew Len, as he is more commonly known, was the first person to document and confirm proof that the new form of ho'oponopono worked. When he saw how ho'oponopono healed his daughter of shingles, when nothing and no one else was able to do so, he was convinced. He studied with Morrnah until her death in 1992, at which time he continued working with ho'oponopono, improving it and simplifying it even further.

It seemed ho'oponopono was destined to remain on the islands of Hawai'i. Until Dr. Joe Vitale, a well-known speaker, writer, and internet marketer caught wind of it. He interviewed and worked with Dr. Hew Len while he wrote his book *Zero Limits*. In *Zero Limits*, Dr. Vitale explains the four simple phrases at the heart of ho'oponopono: I Love You, I'm Sorry, Please Forgive Me, Thank You.

Okay, so ho'oponopono healed shingles. Are there any other examples of its healing powers? As a matter of fact, there is the most amazing story about Dr. Hew Len's tenure at the Hawai'i State Hospital. He oversaw the ward for the criminally insane patients.

These patients were in such a bad mental condition that they had to be chained and shackled, even amongst themselves. The hospital had a hard time maintaining staff because of the fear that one of these criminals might harm them. Dr. Hew Len never saw one patient. And never saw a picture of any patient. Every day, he went into his office where he had a folder about each patient in the ward. He would pull a folder, and practice ho'oponopono.

He did this day in and day out from 1984 until he was no longer needed in 1987. His work was no longer needed because all the patients had been healed and were no longer considered a danger to themselves or anyone else, so they closed the ward.

Dr. Vitale asked Dr. Hew Len how he had healed all those patients without ever seeing a one of them, not even any pictures! Dr. Hew Len replied, "I did not heal them, I healed the part of myself that created them." And therein is the biggest revelation regarding ho'oponopono; that we are all 100-percent responsible for everything in our lives. Everything! Our Three Minds will explain how this can be and will give you a better understanding of how and why ho'oponopono works.

When is the best time to practice ho'oponopono?

Anytime! All the time! Use it before you enter a meeting and again when you leave the meeting. You will likely find you use it the most when you are by yourself, alone with your thoughts. Anytime a less than peaceful thought comes up, say ho'oponopono a few times until the thought is gone. The thought may come back, depending upon the situation that created the thought (a memory). If it does, just continue repeating ho'oponopono until it no longer returns.

Have you ever been in bed, just about to fall asleep, and a thought comes in reminding you of something negative in your day, such as an argument you had with a co-worker? The next thing you know, you can't get to sleep because you keep going around and around replaying the scenario. This is a great time to practice ho'oponopono. Just start repeating it until you stop thinking about your day and you will likely fall peacefully to sleep.

Or you are driving to work, daydreaming as usual, and you suddenly remember that time when you got angry with your dad when you were twelve years old. What!? Where did THAT come from?

It came from the same place all your memories/thoughts come from: your unconscious mind. It is highly likely that this is not the first time this thought has come up, even though it was so long ago. That is a good indicator that whatever the event was that caused the thought had a big impact on you and continues to do so.

In any case, when those kinds of thoughts pop up, just say ho'oponopono around them and it won't be long before you realize those kinds of thoughts are no longer coming into your consciousness.

In fact, you may not even remember what you were saying ho'oponopono about. That is how it works. It cleans your unconscious mind of all the negative energy you have been accumulating over the years. Yes, there will be a period when you are not recognizing the results and it will be, "... just words, they don't mean anything." A friend of mine put it best, saying, "Dammit! They're just words, they don't mean anything. I don't FEEL anything! I don't even know why I keep saying them, but I do." A week later, she was laughing as she recounted that she was saying the words then couldn't remember what she was saying them about. It dawned on her at that moment that ho'oponopono actually does work – and pretty fast, too!

So just stay with it. Ho'oponopono works whether you believe in it or not and whether you feel it or not. So just stay with it and it won't be long before you realize it is actually working for you. You may start to notice that your life is going just a little bit more smoothly, with maybe less drama. You may feel more at ease, and you aren't always getting blasted with all the negative thoughts you used to get. Keep practicing ho'oponopono until it becomes second nature, until it becomes an automatic response to any negative thought or situation that arises.

Where do all these thoughts come from? They come from ourselves, from our unconscious minds, our past experiences. For now, simply remember that thoughts are energy and as such are always coming and going.

You have no doubt heard it said that we are all connected. The ancient Hawai'ians refer to these connections as aka cords. Think of aka cords as very thin cords of energy connecting us one to another. Anytime you come in contact with anything or anyone, you connect with them. Your cord attaches to them and their cord connects to you, creating and maintaining a flow of energy. Even though the amount is minuscule, if you think about all of the people you have come in contact with over the years, you will begin to realize there is a massive energy exchange going on collectively.

Unbeknownst to our conscious minds, we are expending a lot of energy in a lot of different directions. These connections happen so slowly over time and are so subtle, that we do not usually feel them until something pushes them to the surface.

There are situations, however, when we do feel them. Take the breakup of a relationship, for example. Those feelings are usually very strong, and we often have a hard time getting past them. Ho'oponopono will speed that process up and heal the feelings very quickly.
The more of ourselves, our energy, we put into a relationship, the stronger the aka cords are. A full ho'oponopono meditation will guide you through

cutting the cords to everyone and everything you are connected to.

(See http://getpono.com/meditations.htm for this meditation.) Then use the short version, the four statements: "I Love You, I'm Sorry, Please Forgive Me, Thank You" as maintenance. It is good to do the full meditation at least four times per year, or more often if you feel the need, to help keep yourself free of negative aka cords.

This is a very powerful meditation process. There are countless stories about someone cutting cords to someone they knew years ago, and haven't had any contact with, only to receive an email or a phone call from that person, seemingly out of the blue. If this happens, just remember that you now have a choice as to whether you want to reconnect or not.

Ho'oponopono is so simple, so effective, there is no reason NOT to use it at every opportunity. It just takes practice and the more you practice, the sooner it becomes second nature.

Chapter 3 – It Is All in the Mind
Our Three Minds
Conscious, Unconscious, Higher Conscious

"Man's mind may be likened to a garden Which may be cultivated intelligently or allowed to run wild."

-James Allen

To understand how ho'oponopono works, first understand that ho'oponopono is a very powerful, life-transforming meditation. To get the most benefit from the meditation, it helps to understand how it works and why. It works regardless of whether we completely understand why. However, I believe it will be much more powerful and freeing for you if you can understand the how and why.

We first must understand that everything in our lives is 100 percent our own responsibility. This is sometimes difficult for many people to comprehend because of our past and our environment. Society has trained or brainwashed us into thinking that we can cause another person to feel a certain way. The first thing we need to understand is that we are each responsible for our own feelings and no one can make us feel anything. We choose to feel whatever we are feeling. I know, I know, this is a hard nut to crack. It is true though, and the sooner you understand it, accept it, and begin to practice it, the sooner you will be free from feeling controlled by anyone else.

If you take a moment and think about this, I believe you will quickly come to the realization that it is true. You may not like it; however, it is still true. Okay, now that we all know we are responsible for everything that happens in our lives, I hate to do this to you, but it is really important that you also understand and think about what I am about to say.

Not only are we responsible for everything that goes on in our own lives, we are also 100-percent responsible for anything and/or everything we hear/see/read about. In other words, if you are talking with a friend who tells you about something "bad" that happened to someone they know, now, you also have a responsibility for that as well, whatever it is.

So, not only is it difficult to comprehend being 100-percent responsible for everything we do or say ourselves, it is almost impossible to comprehend being responsible for something we knew nothing about five minutes ago, but now that we know about it, we have a responsibility for it!

I know, I know – not only is it hard to understand or comprehend, it is also, at the surface, unsettling to say the least. How on earth can that be? Well, first of all, it is not "on Earth," it is in the Spiritual or unconscious realms.

To help you better understand this; let us take a look at our minds.

The Three Minds

Body, Mind, and Spirit; also referred to as Body, Mind, and Soul:

1. Our Conscious Mind and the illusion of "I."
2. Our Unconscious Mind – many refer to this as the Subconscious; I prefer the term Unconscious; however, they can be used interchangeably.
3. Our Super-Conscious Mind – our Higher Self.

Our Conscious Mind

Our Conscious Mind, known by the Ancient Hawai'ians as Uhane, or Spirit or Soul, is that part of us that commands and/or controls our response and reactions to external events. This is the part of us that wants to be "Right."

Suppose, for example, that you ask someone for help with a project you are working on. You have an amiable discussion and trade ideas and suggestions and arrive at an agreed-upon outcome. When done, you feel whole and complete and in charge; in control.

Now, let's change that scenario a bit and say you are having the same discussion. However, the other person suggests ideas you do not agree with. They simply refuse to see things the way you see them, and you cannot come to an amiable agreement. You start to have feelings of frustration and maybe even anger. You find yourself getting worked up. You are not as calm as when you started. The rational thoughts you would normally have under the previous circumstances are now disrupted by conflicting feelings and even ideas of revenge. You start to take things being said personally, raise your voice, and perhaps even throw up your arms in defeat. Simply because the other person did not agree with you.

What happened? Where did these feelings come from? They come from the Unconscious Mind. Once these feelings start to occur, your Conscious Mind sends thoughts to "Be cool, don't get upset, maintain your calm." Your actual response to the situation will be dependent upon your level of training, and how well you can control your Conscious Mind's impact over your Unconscious Mind. For instance, how well you can control your emotions. This can be very difficult sometimes, due to the Unconscious Mind's release of adrenaline and the fight or flight response, which causes us to react rather than respond.

What is the end result of the above scenario? In the best of circumstances, your Conscious Mind will realize what is happening and you will not react to the negative feelings brought up by your Unconscious Mind; however, more often than not, the opposite will occur. You will more than likely express your dissatisfaction with the situation or person helping you, only to later regret having had a negative reaction to the incident. Oftentimes, after the incident and you have cooled down, you ask yourself, "What happened and why did I get so upset? I wish I had not reacted in such a negative way."

We are aware of our Conscious Minds, and under certain circumstances, we can perceive the presence of our Unconscious Minds. We know the Conscious Mind gives us our inductive reasoning powers, our gifts of speech and will-power. The mission of our Conscious Mind is to take care of the body, to work or earn a living, to make decisions and choices in life, and most importantly, to guide and counsel the Unconscious Mind in its path of evolution.

However, the Conscious Mind has very little memory and must rely upon the Unconscious Mind for the storage, management, and recalling of memories. The Unconscious Mind is the lesser evolved of the three minds. Yet it has excellent memory abilities, remembering everything since the time of creation. It is the seat of all emotions but cannot reason. For reasoning, the Unconscious Mind must rely upon the Conscious Mind.

The Unconscious Mind

Now then, all that being said – this is the key component of the Unconscious Mind, called Unihipili by the Ancient Hawai'ians. It manufactures energy – the Vital Life Force, also referred to as Chi, or Prana, or in the case of ho'oponopono, mana. This energy is created from our environment: the food we eat, the air we breathe, etc. This energy is not only necessary for the vital functions of the body, it is also necessary for the Conscious Mind in order to exercise its free will, and to perform reasoning and thinking.

It is important to understand that the Unconscious Mind is very impressionable and hugely susceptible to suggestion – therefore, the "Power of Suggestion" should not be taken lightly. Interestingly enough, this is also the source of our psychic abilities and where our ability to project, or do astral travel, comes from. This is where our intuition originates. The Unconscious Mind does not make any decisions and does not recognize negative words such as can't, won't, shouldn't, etc. This is why, when you are doing your best to change something like being in debt, you may become deeper in debt. You might say something like, "I don't want to be in debt any longer." What the Unconscious Mind hears, and acts upon, is "debt." It does not recognize the word "don't."

The Unconscious Mind is where our aka cords originate. These cords of energy are projected as thin threads of the psychic, invisible body and attach to other people, animals, or things. These threads carry the mana, the energy, used by the Unconscious Mind to send information to or collect it from the external object. This information is then offered to the Conscious Mind in the form of feelings or intuitive hunches. The Unconscious Mind is also the source of our healing powers. We all have the ability to heal; however, only a few understand and utilize that ability.

The Super-Conscious Mind or Our Higher Self

The Super-Conscious Mind is sometimes referred to as our Guardian Angel, the Super-Consciousness, and the Master within. The Ancient Hawai'ian Kahunas called it the Aumakua, which means, "the utterly trustworthy parental spirit." The Super-Conscious Mind has a superior form of thinking. The Conscious Mind uses reasoning and inductive thinking. The Unconscious Mind uses emotion, memory, and feeling. The Super-Conscious Mind uses a higher form of thinking that includes reasoning, emotion, and memory, or a combination of all three minds.

The Unconscious Mind is a link between the Conscious Mind and the Super-Conscious Mind. The Super-Conscious Mind also has access to Universal Knowledge, sometimes known as the Akashic Records. (We'll save this for another discussion.) For now, think of the Akashic Records as the Library of the Universe. It is the place where all information about everything since the beginning of time is stored.

If and when you have a "Knowing," this comes from the Super-Conscious Mind, which reaches us in a way that the reasoning of the Conscious Mind, as well as the emotion of the Unconscious Mind, cannot overcome.

All three minds are always available to us; however, we cannot normally hear the Super-Conscious Mind unless we quiet the Conscious and Unconscious Minds. Most often, our Super-Conscious Mind is accessed when we are sleeping. We can also access it after prayer, if we remain quiet and actually listen for it.

Meditation is the most reliable way to access our Super-Conscious Mind; this is why it is so important to learn and practice meditation on a regular basis. Most communication from the Super-Conscious Mind comes to us in the form of Intuition, or a feeling or a hunch. It is important to remember that the Super-Conscious Mind is that part of us whose mission is to guide us. Because of this, we must learn to listen to what it is telling us. It is giving us free advice and will never steer us wrong, if we only learn to listen to it. I strongly recommend that you practice meditation on a regular basis.

Happiness

What is the key to happiness? The key to happiness is learning the structure of our three minds and to begin working with them. Through understanding and working with our minds, we can rid and cleanse ourselves of our negative thoughts, feelings, and emotions.

Increasing medical evidence shows that it is the negative thoughts, feelings, and emotions that we keep trapped within that are the cause of most, if not all, of the major chronic illnesses, both mental and physical. These emotions are the result of past events that we have stuffed, that is, we have not dealt with them at the time of their occurrence. We keep them trapped in our Unconscious Minds where they hold large amounts of mana energy. When we do not acknowledge them appropriately, every time something else happens that triggers them, these pools of feelings attempt to come out all at once. This is why oftentimes when something angers us, and we get way angrier than the current circumstance or situation merits, it is because that anger, or negative emotion, has opened the Unconscious Mind and everything that is trapped there attempts to get out, or escape, whether it is related to the current incident or not. Likewise, if you ever feel like you are just wandering through life aimlessly, seemingly without purpose or meaning, it is because you have lost the connection to your Super-Conscious Mind.

Remember, we have three separate and distinct minds: The Conscious, the Unconscious, and the Super-Conscious. Another way to look at it is that our Unconscious Mind is our animal part, the emotions of which need to be tamed and controlled or managed. We need to change the selfish, immature reactions to cooperation. If we do not change our Unconscious Minds and transmute the anger, frustration, aggression, and selfishness into love, tolerance, and compassion, we will continue to ride a roller coaster of chaos, drama, and pain.

The Conscious Mind has the responsibility to guide and counsel the Unconscious Mind; its mission being to help the Unconscious Mind to evolve. The Conscious Mind must also give up its belief that it needs to be right and stop controlling the external world attempting to make it a specific way. Understanding our external world is a result of all three minds. The Conscious Mind must become courageous, generous, unselfish, tolerant, and patient, as well as compassionate. In short, the Conscious Mind must control the negative emotions of the Unconscious Mind.

The Super-Conscious Mind is with us to guide and counsel the lower pair of minds. Its mission is to help them to evolve. The three minds each have different abilities and different priorities. We must find a way to get them to all work together using the best abilities of each: The emotional and memory-bound, deductive Unconscious Mind; the rational, logical, and inductive Conscious Mind, and the superior consciousness of the Super-Conscious Mind. Once again, I cannot stress enough the importance of meditation to bring the Three Minds together harmoniously.

Now then, this is all great and wonderful, right? We understand the Three Minds much better. However, how do we "connect the dots," so to speak? How do we communicate with the Three Minds?

Our normal mode of communication with each other is through speech; however, the Super-Conscious and Unconscious Minds cannot speak. Our gift of speech is specific to the Conscious Mind only. Therefore, we must find another way to communicate with the other minds. Our Super-Conscious and Unconscious Minds do not recognize speech. Their form of communication is through symbols or pictures. This is often done through the use of Tarot Cards, Runes, or Tea Leaves, and other "new age" methods. While these are good ways to communicate, most of them require training.

Once again, I am going to bring up meditation. Through meditation, you use your Conscious Mind to picture or visualize whatever it is that you want to communicate. This works very well, as you may now understand, because you are taking what you see in the external world and internalizing it. If you have not meditated, or have trouble with it, here is a simple exercise that will help you learn to meditate and communicate with your other two minds at the same time.

Set apart some time every day for the sole purpose of communicating with your Super-Conscious Mind and your Unconscious Mind. Preferably, a half-hour; however, if that is too long then start with ten minutes per day, then increase it to twenty minutes, and continue increasing it until you are comfortable with a half-hour. If you do this on a regular basis, you will find that it won't be long, and you will be comfortable sitting quietly for an hour or more. Please though, do yourself a huge favor and set aside at least ten minutes. That is not too much to ask for a happier life, now is it? It is critical that it is quiet. Turn off all electronic devices, no TV or music in the background, no cell phone. Unplug the house phone if there is a possibility that it may ring while you are communicating with Self.

Now, take a couple of deep breaths and relax. Then, tell your Unconscious Mind, in a low voice, that you would like to get to know it better. Begin by asking it to remember fond times from your childhood. Then just sit quietly and notice any memories and feelings that come up.

Do not judge or analyze anything that comes to you; simply notice it. In the beginning, your ego, your Conscious Mind, will likely try to object to you doing this. You may get the thought, "This is ridiculous, why am I talking to myself?" Just let that go and reaffirm to your Unconscious Self that this is important to you and it won't be long before you discover how much valuable information is freely available to you, if you but learn to listen. Keep practicing this until it becomes second nature. In other words, before you make any important decisions, you will stop and quietly ask your Unconscious Mind for help and advice. Once you learn to do this, you will realize that your Super-Conscious Mind will never steer you in a wrong direction. It won't be long, and you will have a new best friend – YOU!

The next thing to remember is that in order to communicate with your Super-Conscious Mind, you must do so through your Unconscious Mind. We do not have a direct connection to the Super-Conscious Mind and cannot normally communicate directly with it; however, once you learn to communicate with the Unconscious Mind, which in turn communicates with the Super-Conscious Mind, it will eventually seem transparent – as if you do have a direct link to your Super-Conscious Mind.

To communicate with your Super-Conscious Mind, you must send your messages through the Unconscious Mind in the form of pictures and feelings. Note, if the Unconscious Mind refuses or ignores the request, no message is sent to the Super-Conscious Mind. That is why many prayers and visualizations do not seem to work; the Unconscious Mind may oppose or have a problem with the request. Therefore, it is so important, even imperative, to get rid of the negative emotions that are stored in the Unconscious Mind. As an example, suppose we want a promotion or a raise at work and we ask the Super-Conscious Mind for help to get it, but the Unconscious Mind is in actuality afraid of taking on the new responsibilities that would come with the promotion or raise due to some past trauma or negative memory. The Unconscious Mind will simply neglect or ignore the request, and the Super-Conscious Mind will never get the message. Therefore, when you are asking for something from the Super-Conscious Mind and not receiving it, ask yourself what could be blocking it in the Unconscious Mind. This is why it is so critical to learn to "talk" to your Unconscious Mind and communicate with it – so you can learn what negativity resides there and needs to be cleansed.

The Super-Conscious Mind, with the cooperation of the Unconscious Mind, can grant us anything we desire, material or immaterial, once we learn how to communicate with it. There are more principles that come into play, but these are covered in another chapter.

To summarize:

We all have Three Minds:
- The Conscious Mind
- The Unconscious Mind
- The Super-Conscious Mind

The Conscious Mind is the self that we present to the world.

The Unconscious Mind remembers everything – everything that has happened in our lives – and is also the source of our emotions or feelings. It can only communicate through images or pictures.

The Super-Conscious Mind can grant us any desire we have and has access to all the knowledge since the beginning of creation, but can only communicate through the Unconscious Mind.

The best ways, although not the only ways, to communicate with the Unconscious Mind are through ho'oponopono and meditation or prayer.

The Unconscious Mind creates mana, or energy, and sends it out to connect with everything we interact with in our lives. The ancient Hawai'ians refer to this connecting mana as aka cords, as I introduced earlier. Herein lies the true power of this ho'oponopono aka-cord-cutting meditation. Through this meditation, we are going to cut the aka cords that are connecting us to our past and that are no longer serving us. When we do this, we then reclaim our energy and allow the others to reclaim their energy.

See http://getpono.com/meditations.htm for this meditation.

When we reclaim our energy and heal ourselves, we also heal the Universe.

e aloha aku (I send aloha)
e aloha mai (I receive aloha)

Ho'oponopono Pule' (Prayer)

Divine Creator, Father, Mother, and Child as one... If I, my family, relatives, and ancestors have offended you, your family, relatives, and ancestors in thoughts, words, deeds, and actions from the beginning of creation to the present, we ask your forgiveness...

Let this cleanse, purify, release, cut all the negative memories, blocks, energies, and vibrations, and transmute these unwanted energies to pure light...

As it is said, it is done, and so it is.

Chapter 4 – From the Top Down

Neuroplasticity
Yes – We Can Rewire the Brain

"Whatever we plant in our subconscious mind and nourish with repetition and emotion will one day become a reality."
-Earl Nightingale

Consistent use of ho'oponopono changes the physiology of our brains through a process known as neuroplasticity. There was a time when people thought that our brains stopped growing at around age thirteen or fourteen, and what you got was what you got. That was it. Scientists have since discovered that the brain is malleable and is always changing based upon our responses to new experiences.

> *Definition: Neural plasticity, which is also known as neuroplasticity, brain plasticity, cortical plasticity, is the changing of the structure, function, and organization of neurons in response to new experiences.*
>
> *Neural plasticity specifically refers to strengthening or weakening nerve connections or adding new nerve cells based on outside experiences.*
> -Dr Madhumita Sen

The first few years of our lives, our brains grow very rapidly. Synapses form, taking in all the external surroundings. At about four years of age, Synapse Pruning begins, and some connections become stronger while others become weaker, and eventually go away completely. How? The stronger ones are continually used and reinforced while the ones that are neglected wither away.

We can think of neuroplasticity as a "use it or lose it" scenario. That is not actually the case as there is so much more going on in the background. However, if we think of it that way, we are more apt to apply changes. The more we reinforce our beliefs by our thoughts, feelings, words, actions, and deeds, the stronger they become in our brains. We essentially become a product of our environment, changing as our environments change.

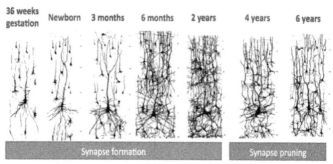

Fig. 3-2. Synaptic Formation/Pruning
https://itsnotwhatitswhy.wordpress.com/2015/08/05/bending-your-brain-

For example, when we move to another place and the speech pattern is different, over time we may find ourselves speaking the same way the locals speak. When I moved from Kansas City, Missouri, to upstate New York, I was often teased about my accent. I had a bit of a Southern drawl and within a few years, the teasing stopped because I had assimilated the New York accent into my speech. The same thing happened when I moved to Phoenix, Arizona. The first couple of years, I often heard, "Where are you from?" That question faded away over time indicating that I was now a "local." The same thing happens with different languages. I am learning the Hawai'ian language via words and phrases, basically without even trying because I hear them often enough and am incorporating them into my vocabulary.

Neuroplasticity is simply practice and repetition.

The more we practice something, the more it changes our brain and we come to a point where we no longer must focus all of our attention on whatever we are practicing.

Driving is a good example. When we first start learning to drive, it is a challenge remembering to keep two hands on the wheel, pushing the clutch in before shifting gears, which pedal is the brake and which is the clutch, how to use the mirrors, etc.

Within a very short time, that all becomes automatic and we do not really think about what needs to be done. We just do it, automatically. Therefore, we can talk or text on cell phones, put on makeup, eat, drink, and be merry, all while we are driving. We no longer need to pay so much attention to how hard to press the gas pedal, and when to apply the brake. We have done it enough times that we no longer have to focus on it, allowing us to do other things as we drive. There is a caveat here, however. Psychology 101 teaches us that we can only concentrate on one thing at a time, so even though we "think" we are multi-tasking, we truly are not. If our attention is on the phone or looking at the food we are eating, we may not see the brake lights in front of us in time. So even though we are capable of driving and texting, it does not mean that we should.

This applies to everything we do. The more we repeat (practice) something, the sooner it becomes automatic. What we fail to recognize is that whether we are constantly being degraded or loved, the repetition is creating new axons, dendrites, etc., in our brains. They continue to get stronger to the point that when we encounter a similar situation elsewhere, we react the same way as during the original encounter, because that reaction was what worked for us in the earlier situation.

However, sometimes that learned reaction is not appropriate under different circumstances. We see this in our relationships as we grow older. One person comes from an environment of strife and struggle, with many insults and degradation, while another person comes from one of love and joy with lots of hugs and praise. These two types of people may meet and have common interests, but as they move through their relationship, they begin to notice differences in how they react to similar situations.

One person may hear something and be insulted by it, while the other person has no reaction to it at all. The person from the loving environment may be very easily offended by something as simple as a loud voice, while the person from the degrading paradigm may think nothing of it. On the flip side, the degraded person may feel embarrassed at receiving praise and compliments, while the well-loved person may not react in the same way at all.

The interesting question about this kind of scenario is "How can two people from such diverse paradigms even come together in the first place?" Why is it that opposites seem to attract? This will be explained in *Chapter 5: Come to Me ~ Calling and Feeding*. The simple answer is that we attract that which we need, to show us how to become the best self we can be.

Why does this happen? How does neuroplasticity play into this kind of scenario?

Let us refer to the first six years of growth and remember how the brain develops. It takes in everything for the first three to four years, then it starts to prune itself of the unused input and retains only the things that are consistently repeated. Fast forward to adulthood and we are now going to do what I call conscious pruning. Another way to say this might be pruning with intent.

The following figures represent a rudimentary picture of the neural pathways in our brains.

Looking at Figure 3-3, let us imagine we have a thought about an upcoming bill, and we are not sure how we will be able to pay it. This can create thoughts and feelings of worry. Figure 3-4 shows the pathway getting thicker and stronger with repeated worrying.

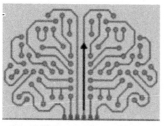 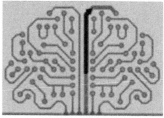

Fig. 3-3. Thought/ Feeling (worry) · Copyright (c) Santis¶   Fig. 3-4. Thought/ Feeling (worry) · Copyright (c) Santis¶

This will continue until worry becomes our dominant go-to for similar situations. As we know, what we worry about comes to pass. How do we stop the worry and the programming?

The best way I have found is to start saying ho'oponopono as soon as possible. Note the white stripe in Figure 3-5. In Figure 3-6 the white stripe is getting thicker and stronger every time we say it.

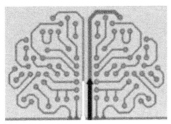

Fig. 3-5. · Add ho'oponopono
Copyright (c) Sentis

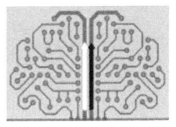

Fig. 3-6. · Continue ho'oponopono
Copyright (c) Sentis

As we continue to repeat it, notice how the white side is getting bigger and stronger, and the black stripe (worry) is getting smaller in Figure 3-7. As we continue saying ho'oponopono, and as you can see in Figure 3-8, the worry (the black stripe) goes away completely.

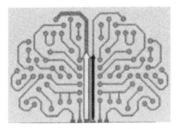

Fig. 3-7. · Worry diminishing
Copyright (c) Sentis

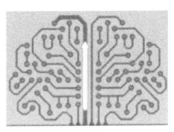

Fig. 3-8. · Worry replaced
Copyright (c) Sentis

The same process is used to clean and clear any memory that is no longer serving our higher good.

This is an example of how neuroplasticity works. Once we understand it, we can now begin to reform our brains consciously, on purpose, and with intent. We will take a closer look at this process in more detail in subsequent chapters and in case studies.

Summary: Neuroplasticity shows us that repeated thoughts become habits which become automatic responses. If we do not like our habits and automatic responses, we now know it is possible to change them. How we do that is the subject of this book.

Chapter 5 – Come to Me

Calling and Feeding
A Different View of the Law of Attraction

*"How you vibrate is what the universe
echoes back to you in every moment."*
-Panache

Imagine that you see a stray cat and you decide that
you want to take it in as a pet. How do you do that?
You put some food out, you feed it, and you call it
in. Sure enough, it works, and the cat starts coming
closer. Then one day, you look outside, and you
have eight cats eating the food you put out! "Oy
vey! I only want one cat!" What do you do? You
stop feeding and calling the cats. Then you
gradually put more food out and the cat you
wanted to begin with comes back. You continue
monitoring and feeding, calling the cat you want to
you until it becomes your pet.

Our feelings are cat food!

Every feeling we have is feeding the Universe,
calling for more of the same. We never get just the
feeling; rather, we get opportunities to experience
the feeling(s) again. Therefore, we often find
ourselves in uncomfortable situations, saying,
"How did I get in this situation? AGAIN?!" It is
because we continue to have the feelings that create
that situation. This pattern continues until we clean

and clear those feelings and again, ask ourselves, "How did I create this for myself, and why?"

As with the other 7 Laws of the Universe (see Appendix 2) – the Law of Attraction is always working and immutable. We always get what we ask for! The challenge is that we forget, or do not realize, that when we are stomping our feet and throwing a fit, we are asking (feeding). The more we express our feelings (calling), the more and faster we get what we are asking for. Remember, there is no good or bad as far as the Universe goes – everything just IS! Something is only good or bad because we compare it to something else (the Third Law).

Every feeling we have is asking for more of the same. This is another place where ho'oponopono is so powerful. Whenever we are feeling any of the lower vibrational feelings, say ho'oponopono until the feeling dissipates. We do not know how long it will take for the Universe to respond (Law of Gender), and how it will show up, but what we do know is that it WILL respond. So, the sooner we negate those low vibrational feelings in the moment, the less chance they have of coming back.

If or when those feelings do return, we now know how to heal them. Simply repeat ho'oponopono a few times and ask ourselves, "How did I create this for myself, and why?"

Repeating ho'oponopono over and over as a mantra will more often than not guide us to the answers. Then we may take responsibility, love ourselves, apologize to ourselves, forgive ourselves, and come into the gratitude for the experience(s) and the lesson(s) learned.

I love you
I am sorry
Please forgive me
Thank you

Whenever we feel any of these feelings, repeat ho'oponopono over and over, and very quickly the feelings will dissipate, and we will begin to feel better.

The sooner we can start saying the words, the less chance we have of reacting. Instead, we learn to respond to a situation or circumstance. Response is predominantly in the higher vibrational feelings while reaction is typically in these lower vibrational feelings. Remember that our feelings are just that – ours! No one can "make" us feel anything – it is always a choice.

Chapter 6 – Our Driving Force

Feelings

Connect to the Unconscious

"Unexpressed emotions will never die they are buried alive and will come forth later in uglier ways."

-Freud

I first came across this list of feelings while reading *Ask and It Is Given* by Esther and Jerry Hicks with the teachings of Abraham. The basic premise of their book is that we all want to be at the top of Joy/Knowledge/etc. Most of us spend a lot of time in the, what I call, lower vibrational energies or feelings. Usually between Frustration and Jealousy, with bouts of lower and higher feelings. How do we get to the top? Incrementally.

Our biggest obstacle is, of course, ourselves – we get in our own way. The trick is to come up the spiral in steps. For example, Revenge feels better than Hatred/Rage and Anger feels better than Revenge, and Discouragement is better than Anger, etc.

I highly recommend you right-click and download this image from getpono.com/feelings.htm, save it, print it, and hang it on your refrigerator or someplace you will see it every day. It is a very simple way to check in with self. Whatever you are feeling when you pass the poster may or may not be very strong, but if you walk out the door feeling any of the lower vibrational feelings, you will likely find yourself in situations or circumstances that will increase the intensity of those feelings.

This is a very useful tool to monitor our feelings and is instrumental in helping us better understand ho'oponopono. The more we practice and use ho'oponopono, the more we become consciously aware of our unconscious, our feelings.

I have this posted on my refrigerator, so I see it every day. However, like most everything else in our homes, after the newness wears off, we no longer notice it as much.

Our unconscious minds always see everything in our current environment (and much more, but that is another topic).

Here's what I notice is happening. I am in the upper spiral probably 90 percent of the time. Even when I think I am in the state of peace, enthusiasm, joy, etc., with nothing consciously bothering me at the moment, I will pass by this poster or start to open the refrigerator.

For some unknown reason, my eyes will be drawn to one of the lower vibrational feelings – let's say disappointment, for example. What I have realized over time is when that happens, that is my unconscious mind showing me there is something for me to clear. So, I pause for a moment and ask

myself, "What am I disappointed about?" As I think about it, it does not take long for me to remember something that happened yesterday that was disappointing. Because ho'oponopono is so automatic for me, I practiced it at the time of the disappointment, and of course, that disappointment dissipated in that moment. This is why I call it the Language of Ho'oponopono – my unconscious mind remembered it, as it remembers everything from the beginning of creation. It was doing its best to show me that there was still some cleaning/clearing to be done at a deeper level by diverting my eyes to a specific area on the poster. If I have the time in that moment (fifteen minutes to a half-hour), I will delve into it at a deeper level. How do I do that?

I first do some "ha breathing" – usually four ha breaths followed by a fifth breath where I purse my lips like I am exhaling through a straw, letting the air out, yet not forcing it out. "Ha" means breath in Hawai'ian. Ha breathing is taking a deep breath into our na'au (our core – located just below the navel) and exhaling twice as long, making a "haaa" sound. This is a very relaxing and powerful breathing technique. And, as with ho'oponopono, it's very simple, deep breathing into our abdomen. No need to count or focus on a pattern, just breathe.

This very quickly brings me into a meditative state and into the moment. I then tune into that feeling of disappointment and ask myself, "Where is this coming from? How did I create this for myself, and why?" And of course, the first thing I remember is the situation from yesterday. But I continue asking myself, "When did I feel this previously relative to what initiated it?" And lo and behold, sure enough, another memory pops up from a similar circumstance from my past. I continue doing this, looking for the first time I remember ever feeling this disappointment – "this" disappointment relating to what triggered the memory in the first place. I have a lot of disappointment stuff in my past and the idea that I can clean/ clear it all at once is ludicrous; however, I can clear it as it relates to the current situation or circumstance.

For example, say my disappointment came from someone else telling me they would give me a ride to an appointment, and they were late picking me up causing me to miss my appointment. So how did I create this? I was not the one that made me late. I created it because I asked a friend who I know is always late and I did not take that into consideration.

For example, I did not ask them to pick me up a half-hour earlier than I needed to be picked up. This would likely have solved the late situation. They would have been late per our agreement, but I would have made my appointment on time. And yes, there is usually anger associated with any disappointment, but if we follow the reasons back, we will find that it is usually self-imposed.

In the above situation, yes, I had a moment of anger, said ho'oponopono, and very quickly realized the anger was at myself in the form of, "Damn, I know they are always late and I forgot about that when I asked." The benefit of practicing ho'oponopono this way is that it stops the low-vibrational feelings from getting bigger in the moment. By the time the person picked me up, I was already over the anger and able to come back to a place of gratitude for their help. That felt much better than what used to be my usual response of yelling or speaking harshly to them about how they made me miss my appointment and projecting MY feelings on to them.

What happens when I do that and project my feelings onto them? The other person may immediately get more defensive. They are likely already defensive by being late, so my projecting on them just adds to it. Because of our paradigms, we both go into a low-vibrational argument because that is what we know. Whereas, by practicing ho'oponopono first and owning my own feelings, there was no projection and it was much easier to stay in the gratitude. Plus, it is just hard for me to be mad at a person I asked to do me a favor anyway.

Remember, ho'oponopono cleaning/clearing is a lifelong process and we will never reach the end and be 100-percent clean and clear. However, the more we do it, the better we feel, and the more love, humility, compassion, and gratitude we notice in our lives.

So, sure enough, I can recognize a time a couple of years ago when I heard a similar comment that at that time really pissed me off. At that point, I bring that memory to the forefront and ask myself, "How did I create that for myself, and why?" As I delve into the memory, it is now simple for me to understand how I created it, accept responsibility for it, love myself, apologize for creating the situation/circumstance and for hurting the other person. I am then able to forgive myself for doing so, now understanding why it happened the way it did at that time and giving thanks for the love and forgiveness.

Having cleared that memory, the next time I walk by the chart and "think" I am in the upper spiral, I notice that my eyes actually go to one of the feelings in the upper spiral – proving, to me anyway, that I have indeed cleared that memory. Remembering three key concepts:

- All judgment is self-judgment.
- There can be no forgiveness without understanding.
- There will be many more similar opportunities to continue clearing/cleaning.

Our feelings are our driving force. Everything we do is connected to how we feel and every situation or circumstance we find ourselves in is because of our feelings.

Chapter 7 – From the Bottom Up

Depression
Hopeless, Helpless, Powerless

"You may have to fight a battle more than once to win it."

\- Margaret Thatcher

I wrote the following article last year in response to a flurry of suicide posts on Facebook:

I was contemplating suicide, again, about 15 years ago – I say again because I did it back in 1991 successfully, but the hospital brought me back somehow. Anyway, 10-15ish years ago when I was contemplating suicide again, I was blessed to have learned a little mantra that ultimately not only saved my life, but has actually given me a life of peace, joy, and love – always! Today suicide never even comes up until I see it on posts or hear about it. I no longer can even fathom the idea.

What is the mantra?

Ho'oponopono
I love you
I am sorry
Please forgive me
Thank you

I just started saying these words over and over and over again. At that time I did not understand it and it did not make much sense. But it felt good. It felt better than any other thought I had been having at the time, so I just kept saying it over and over, all the time. It was not long before an opportunity showed itself and I started to have a glimmer of hope again – something I had completely lost. And that is perhaps the biggest catalyst for suicide – when we lose all hope.

I did not really understand what was happening, I just kept saying ho'oponopono over and over and my life started changing and becoming so much better, and very quickly. At that time I did not yet equate a better life to ho'oponopono. I thought it was some kind of a miraculous coincidence.

So, life quickly returned to normal (whatever that is LoL) and as my life got better, I slowly stopped saying ho'oponopono as much – ugh – live 'n' learn. In 2011 I found myself homeless and jobless, but not hopeless. I started saying ho'oponopono again and within a month I got an awesome job that I still have and love. Six months later I won an award at work and three months after that I received a promotion. Long story. A little shorter... within a year I received 3 awards, 2 promotions, and moved to Hawai'i where I am now. Today I have the most amazing ohana (family). I have learned to go where I am celebrated, not tolerated. I have learned what unconditional love really means. We throw that term around a lot, but most of us do not truly understand it. Ho'oponopono gives us that understanding.

If you are contemplating suicide or know someone who is, start repeating ho'oponopono and have them say ho'oponopono ... over and over and over and over again – make it an endless loop in the back of your mind.

I have seen ho'oponopono prevent suicide a few times this past year – when nothing else was working. Ho'oponopono has always worked!!!

"I started to have a glimmer of hope again – something I had completely lost" – and that is perhaps the biggest catalyst for suicide: when we lose all hope.

Hope: That seems to be what it all boils down to, at least for me, and many others I have worked with. It got to a point of pure, utter, hopelessness.

That is when I found myself totally and completely helpless, hopeless, and with no way out. It seemed that no matter which way I turned; it was a dead-end. It seemed that it was always going to end badly.

Do these internal messages sound familiar?

"Nobody listens, nobody cares. I have tried to talk to numerous people, and they all have more important things to do, more important places to be. Why can't they see? They just don't care, yet they say they love me, but they don't show it."

"Every time I try to talk to her about how I feel, she gets angry, or worse, starts teasing me! Whenever I call my friends, and I use that term loosely, they are busy and say they will call me back, but they never do!"

"I want to just quit this relationship, but I don't know how to get out of it gracefully. And, even if I could, I don't have enough money to get my own place. My job sucks! I work for peanuts doing something I don't even like doing! Why do I keep doing this? Why can't I get out of this vicious cycle? Everywhere I turn, things just turn out horribly!"

"I just can't do it any longer! This has been going on for weeks, months – maybe years! I bet they will wish they had listened when I am gone! Oh hell, who am I kidding, they probably won't even know I am gone for days – well, unless they need something!"

"I am done!! I just can't do it anymore!!!"

And so it went. I do not remember the exact day, but it was in 1991. I will not go into too many details for obvious reasons – this is a book about how to heal, not how to die! Suffice it to say that I did actually experience the tunnel I had always heard about with the light at the end. The light was much different than had been described or I had imagined. Such that it is very difficult to describe, but I will do my best:

The light started out round and as I got closer it became more oblong and undulating, first stretching left to right, then stretching top to bottom and spinning the entire time – more like an orb. I could kind of see through, or into it, but could not make out what was inside, or beyond. The feeling was of immense love and peace and freedom. The closer I got to the light, the more intense the feelings became, and I believe this is when I first experienced what unconditional love truly feels like. Then suddenly I saw very bright white stripes flashing by. It took a bit – I have no idea how long. The white stripes were fluorescent lights and I was lying on a gurney being wheeled down a hallway in a hospital. And then I do not remember anything else until I was admitted to the Behavioral Sciences Unit at the hospital. I was released the next day after an interview with a psychiatrist when I told him, "I just drank too much. If I don't drink so much, I do not get suicidal." His reply, "Well, just don't drink so much. I don't see any reason to keep you." I was discharged.

I never tried suicide again after that. A fleeting thought would come in once in a great while and I would just laugh and remind myself that it is apparently no longer an option for me.

Ten to fifteen years later, I found myself contemplating suicide again. I was in a very similar situation – a relationship that was not working, unemployed ... same scenario, different people and location, but the feelings were the same.

That is what we want to understand, the feelings. The people and places can change, but the feelings remain the same. It is not the people or the places that cause us to feel the way we do. The way we feel is 100 percent our responsibility. Our feelings are always our choice – again, from learned behavior, which we will cover in detail in subsequent chapters.

Herein lies the difficulty. Most of us are taught from a young age that someone else can make you feel a certain way. And we are shown how that can be so. We are also inundated with that concept in the media, particularly television sitcoms. How many sitcoms often have remarks like? "You make me feel like an idiot!" or "You make me feel so small!" Many of us have heard this at home, as well, which is why the sitcoms are so relatable.

Many of us are used to this kind of behavior. We grew up with it. When we listen to others, we sometimes hear things like, "My Dad made me feel so small and insignificant." Or "My Mom was always making me feel bad about my weight."

"You make me feel_!" This is simply not true. No one can make us feel anything and we cannot make anyone else feel anything! I know, this is a hard concept to grasp, at first. However, the more we practice ho'oponopono, the more we come to understand. *Chapter 4: From the Top Down ~ Neuroplasticity* explains how and why this happens. Suffice to say that we all "choose" to feel whatever we are feeling, based upon our own paradigm. It is learned behavior.

This is when ho'oponopono becomes so powerful.

> I love you
> I am sorry
> Please forgive me
> Thank you

Ho'oponopono teaches us that each one of us is 100-percent responsible for everything in our lives. Always has been and always will be. We will delve deeper into where it came from, why it works, and how it works. We will walk through processes to take ho'oponopono to its deepest levels as we progress through this book.

For now, let's finish my story of contemplating suicide approximately fifteen years ago. As I said, I again reached my limits and could not fathom a way out, but I had heard about ho'oponopono and at some point, I just started repeating it to myself. Over and over and over, pretty much nonstop. The more I continued to say it, the better I started to feel.

First and foremost, I began to experience hope again. Something I thought I had lost. Again.

For myself and numerous others whom I have spoken with about suicide, the one common denominator was that each of us lost all hope. We were at the bottom of the spiral. Suffice it to say that feelings of fear, grief, depression, powerlessness, or victimhood are essentially forms of hopelessness. It feels as if there is nowhere else to turn. Always look for the blessings in anything that is happening. The blessing here is that to feel better, there is no place to go but up. Once we have just a little bit of hope, we can pull ourselves out of the black hole.

Chapter 8 – Make the Agreement

The Four Agreements
by Don Miguel Ruiz

"We only see what we want to see; we only hear what we want to hear. Our belief system is just like a mirror that only shows us what we believe."

-Don Miguel Ruiz

As I begin this chapter, I am not sure which has had a bigger impact on my life, The Four Agreements or ho'oponopono; however, when we combine the two? Hang on, or fasten your seatbelt, as I so often say: We are in for a ride.

The Four Agreements and ho'oponopono are two of the simplest practices that I know of after forty years of studying ancient texts, metaphysics, mysticism, quantum physics, etc. While they are simple in concept, they are the hardest things I have learned to live by.

The Four Agreements:

- Be impeccable with your word
- Don't take anything personally
- Don't make any assumptions
- Always do your best

The Four Agreements book is a MUST READ if you want to expedite your ho'oponopono practice. Also know that consistent practice of ho'oponopono becomes a lifestyle. I am seeing it happen more and more with myself and so many others, and it is so gratifying! It brings us to live in our own truth, first and foremost.

If our truth does not match someone else's truth, we talk story about it so we can better understand the differences. We come to a place of unconditional love for self and of self, and from there we can then love another unconditionally. When we are in unconditional love for one another, we more easily speak our truth while at the same time being able to keep an open mind to someone else's truth. More often than not, there is a middle ground that works for all parties. YaY!

Be Impeccable with Your Word

This is a good start and the more you pay attention to this and live by it, the more you realize it is much bigger than just "say what you mean, mean what you say." I encourage you to practice as much as you can. Just ask yourself if you are going against your word if you suddenly decide to change plans at the last minute.

> *I go back and forth to Los Angeles, California, to do Ho'oponopono Talk Story sessions, and about a year ago, I had four sessions scheduled*

in a ten-day period. Three were tentative, but seemed good, the fourth one was a definite.

I came back to the island, and the week I was to leave to return to L.A. to do the sessions, the three tentative sessions did not work out. I was in a dilemma. I had the one session that was booked with my friend Robin in Huntington Beach. I believe it was on a Friday and I did not get confirmation of the others until two days before that. Ugh! So, what do I do? Do I fly over and rent a car for one workshop, or should I cancel it? I already knew what I was going to do, but I did what most all of us do. I checked in with people I know love me and will tell me the truth. Every person I talked to about it said, "Cancel it. He will understand since the other sessions fell through." Funny thing is, there was a brief moment when I actually considered that idea after hearing it enough times. Long story shorter, I "bit the bullet" and flew over to do the session knowing it was what I had to do. I ended up doing four sessions in a week anyway, which was more than I expected, so YaY! Listen to your heart!

There are a multitude of lessons or things to pay attention to in the story above. First, I want to talk about *Be Impeccable With Your Word*, yeah? I told Robin I would be at his shop, The Living Temple, on a specific day at a specific time. Yes, one person was simple to cancel or reschedule. However, take into consideration that he sent out a mass email to his list promoting the event. A cancellation would be a lot of extra work and there would undoubtedly be some who did not receive the cancellation notice and would show up to no event – not good for either of us. So, like I said, I knew right away what I was going to do, but some of my old paradigm programming hiding in my unconscious mind found a way to present itself for healing. That is what prompted me to ask around about "the right thing to do."

What else did I learn from that? That it is a pretty common thing we do. If there is something we do not particularly want to do, we may ask our friends what they think and we are usually pretty good at framing it, so it sounds like a good idea to not do it. And we often get agreement that it is okay to do it the easier way.

Why is this so important?

Because ho'oponopono teaches us that each one of us is 100-percent responsible for ourselves; we always have been and always will be. When we come to that realization, embody and embrace it, there is no more blame. If and when we take full responsibility for ourselves, all of ourselves, we can no longer blame anyone or anything else for our consequences.

The above scenario of asking around until we get the answers we want to hear is our subtle way of shifting responsibility to others. If it goes poorly, we can then say, "Well dang, I asked around, I talked to a bunch of people, and they all said it was a good idea."

Many say, "That is old behavior"; however, if we are doing it today, it is not old, now is it? It is based on older memories and older feelings that likely were stuffed, not able to be expressed in the moment.

The main point here is that when we feel ourselves starting to ask others about how we should proceed with something, we should ask ourselves, "Why do I need another opinion?" Sometimes we truly do want other opinions, so it is important to answer with complete honesty and transparency. Even though I followed through on the old paradigm memories/feelings and asked numerous people what they thought I should do, I did not follow through with their answers even though they all said to cancel. Why not? One word: INTEGRITY!

I love how James Allen describes integrity in his book, *As a Man Thinketh, The Keepsake Edition* (Page 135).

> *"For the man of integrity is in line with the fixed laws of things – not only with the fundamental principles on which human society rests, but with the laws which hold the vast universe together. Who shall set these at naught? Who then shall undermine the man of unblemished integrity? He is like a strong tree*

*whose roots are fed by the perennial springs,
and which not tempest can lay low."*

As if that is not enough, he goes on to say:

*"To be complete and strong, integrity must
embrace the whole man, and extend to all the
details of his life; and it must be so thorough and
permanent as to withstand all temptations to
swerve into compromise. To fail in one point is
to fail in all, and to admit, under stress, a
compromise with falsehood, howsoever
necessary and insignificant it may appear, is to
throw down the shield of integrity, and to stand
exposed to the onslaughts of evil."*

We now better understand the importance and
depth of the first agreement: "Be Impeccable With
Your Word." Does this help give a better
understanding of the importance of that? I certainly
hope so, because for me integrity has become the
cornerstone of my life, my foundation, if you will.
It seems that the strength of our integrity is pretty
much directly proportionate to how well we are
impeccable with our word.

[1]It is really just as simple as asking ourselves, "Am
I being impeccable with my word?" And if we still
are not sure, which is highly unlikely, simply
repeat ho'oponopono a few times, and more often

---

[1] *Note:* As a Man Thinketh *was published in 1903, hence the gender-specific
nature of the book; it is in the public domain and may be downloaded as a
PDF for free.*

than not, we "feel" the truth. Ho'oponopono is our direct connection to our unconscious mind and brings us fully into our hearts when practiced consistently. And when we are living from our hearts, we are living in our truth.

I strongly encourage you to pay more attention to being impeccable with your word. Even, or maybe especially, with the small things like being on time. Are you someone who is always on time or early? If so, why? Is it because you do what you say you will when you say you will? Or is it out of fear of what someone else might think of you if you are late? If your answer is the former, then YaY! Keep it up! If your answer is the latter, then keep reading!

Also notice when others are asking you for advice about how to handle a similar situation. Are they looking for a scapegoat to blame if it does not work out as they hope? So, when it all falls apart, they can say, "I don't know, so and so said ... or everyone said ..." and immediately they are out of integrity, and they shake their own foundation.

I love you, I am sorry, please forgive me, thank you. I love you, I am sorry, please forgive me, thank you. I love you, I am sorry, please forgive me, thank you will always lead us to our truth. Let me restate that. In my experience, repetition of ho'oponopono always leads me to my truth. My heart and I hear the same from many others.

Got it? Good! *Always Do Your Best* is the fourth agreement. So always do your best to be impeccable with your word and stay in your highest integrity. The more we stay in our highest integrity, the easier it is to live to the second agreement:

Do not take anything personally.

I sometimes say it a different way: "What other people think of me is none of my business."

I want to take a deeper look at this, as taking things personally is perhaps our biggest struggle, our biggest challenge to overcome. Most of us grew up in a "What will people think?" mindset, so we learn early on to make sure we look like a million bucks before we leave the house, lest we be judged.

One of the most difficult things we learn to overcome is to believe that we can make others responsible for our feelings. As we discussed earlier, this is continually reinforced in the media on a daily basis, where we often hear lines such as, "You make me feel like_____." Because it wears the mask of entertainment, we do not think much about it. However, remember from neuroplasticity that repetition is how we build stronger pathways in our brains until they become automatic in nature. This is important to understand because the more we are inundated with that kind of programming, the more automatic our reactions are, because they are continually strengthened within our psyche.

What happens when we take something personally? The initial reaction is usually a fight or flight reaction. We go into defense mode, ready to defend ourselves. It also makes us very vulnerable and we do whatever we can to escape that feeling. We have been taught to hide our vulnerability, as it is a sign of weakness. So, we start to argue and defend ourselves, and our automatic programming kicks in. You know, the one that we made stronger by watching television. Then we start blaming someone or something else for our behavior, only to find out later that whatever the other person was spouting off about had nothing to do with us. They were just expressing their feelings in that moment and it felt like they were saying it to us.

Whatever they are angry or upset about is theirs, not ours, even though it felt like they were projecting their feelings toward us. What typically happens is that we say or do something that triggers a response in someone else, and in their reactive moment, they defend themselves by doing their best to put their feelings upon us. Not knowing any better, we take their feelings on, and think that they are attacking us. Then we start to defend ourselves and here we go again down the negative, low-vibrational rabbit hole.

All judgment is self-judgment!

I recommend the following when you catch yourself taking something personally. First, say ho'oponopono and bring yourself into a responsive state rather than staying reactive. Then ask yourself, "Why am I taking this personally? Is it truly about me?" Usually it is not. However, there is something that does feel familiar, so it makes it more difficult to just brush it off. In the moment, it is usually just enough to say ho'oponopono to get out of the reactive state. Then later when you have time, you can start to understand why you took something personally.

Here is the process I use when I am working on a personal issue. It really does not matter what the situation is, but for now I will focus on the second agreement: Do not take anything personally.

What happens when we take something personally? How does it feel? Feel into what that feels like for you. For me, the biggest thing about it is "I am not good enough." This is ridiculous, of course. However, that is my paradigm programming and for many years I did not know better. I spent twenty-five or so years drinking because when I had a few drinks, I felt like " somebody" and could talk more easily with people. This is very common, and drugs are often also a part of that picture. I will go into more detail in *Chapter 12: Chasing the Dragon ~ Addiction.*

For example, when someone says something like, "You are a worthless! You are never going to amount to anything!" What is your reaction to that statement? Have you ever heard statements like that? Or have you said them? They hurt. What happens here, using my own programming as an example, is that when I heard derogatory statements growing up, I believed them. You know, when we hear those words from someone we respect, we tend to take what they say to heart. There is more to this story which I will cover in *Chapter 11: Just Make It Go Away ~ Chronic Pain.*

For me, the degree to which I may take something personally is directly proportional to how much respect I have for the person. There are times when it behooves us to listen to something that may be hard for us to hear. That being said, again it comes down to how much do I respect that person — are they saying this for my best interest, out of love for me, or attacking me to make themselves feel better?

So, as it happened, I heard a lot of that growing up, enough so that I believed I was worthless and would never amount to anything. I proceeded to spend the next twenty-five years proving it true by drinking a lot and becoming an alcoholic.

What happens after we hear statements like that for a long period is that they become ingrained to the point where we actually no longer really hear the words. We become attuned to the tone of the voice and then every time we hear that vocal tone, we hear "You are worthless!" I learned this when I healed that memory, and thirty years of chronic back pain was healed along with it. I realized, in that moment, that I most likely only heard it that one time. But I took it to heart so strongly that every time my Dad was angry and raised his voice, I heard, "You are worthless!" This continued for many years. If someone raised their voice at me, I took it personally, and my immediate feeling was worthlessness.

Since healing that and doing my best to live to the Four Agreements and ho'oponopono, it is very rare that I take anything personally any longer. It still happens every once in a while, but I immediately repeat ho'oponopono a few times, then ask myself:

"Why am I taking this personally? Is it really about me, or am I taking on someone else's feelings?"

More often than not, I find it to be the latter. I rarely take things personally, but when I do it is because someone I have a great deal of respect for is doing their best to help me see something within myself. Then I may want to look at it all a little deeper and maybe change, maybe not, but at least I can be aware of the behavior. I count those occasions as major blessings. The more we heal that which no longer serves our higher purpose, the more we come to know freedom, peace, serenity, and joy. Most importantly, we come to love ourselves unconditionally.

A diligent practice of ho'oponopono and the Four Agreements will bring you to that unconditional love for self. Once you have that, then, and only then, can you love anyone else unconditionally. Yes, as with all other teachings, it starts within.

The third agreement is:

Do not make assumptions.

This is actually very tricky. We often make assumptions without knowing we are doing so. How do you know? Disappointment. Think about that a bit. How many times have you been disappointed only to realize it was because of an assumption you did not know you made? Ugh – quite often for me; however, I am noticing a drastic drop in disappointments, indicating that I am making far fewer assumptions.

Pay attention to when you take things personally, too. My experience shows me that whenever I take something personally, there was an assumption in the mix somewhere, yeah? You too? Think about it.

Repeat ho'oponopono and ask, "Did I make an assumption somewhere?"

> I love you
> I am sorry
> Please forgive me
> Thank you

And usually by the third or fourth repetition, the answer bubbles up from our unconscious. It could be "I assumed they were talking about me." Watch for the hidden assuming words like "think/thought," as in, "I thought they were talking about me." We all make assumptions all the time because often, that is just the way it has always been done.

Holiday Dinner

Imagine: The whole family, four generations, is gathered for a holiday dinner. Mom is in the kitchen about to put a big ham in the oven, talking story with her daughter. She cuts a couple of inches off of each end of the ham before she puts it in the pan to put in the oven. The daughter asks, "Mom, why did you cut off pieces of the ham from both sides? Mom replies, "I do not know, that is just the way it has always been done. Your grandmother is in the dining room, she probably knows."

So, the daughter goes into the dining room and asks, "Grandma, Mom was putting the ham in the oven and before she did so she cut a couple of inches off of either side before she put it in. She does not know why she does that, she said you would probably know. Do you know why she cuts off part of the ham before putting it in the oven?"

Grandma answers, "No, sweetie, I do not know why. That is just the way it has always been done. Your great-grandmother is in the living room, she MUST know."

The daughter goes into the living room and asks, "Great-Grandma, Mom just cut off a couple of inches from each end of the ham before she put it in the oven and she does not know why she does that. Grandma does not know why, and you MUST know why. Do you know why she does that?"

Great-Grandma responds, "Why no, sweetie, I do not know why she is doing that. If you can find out, will you please let me know? Back in my day, the ovens and pans were much smaller, and the ham would not fit, so rather than cut one big hunk off of one end, I cut a little off of each end so the ham would fit in the oven. Today they have these huge ovens and pans so I do not understand why they are still doing that!"

"That is just the way it has always been done."

If and when we hear this, it is almost a guaranteed assumption being made. Because that is the way it has always been done in our family, we assume it is the same for every family. That is, until we experience it differently. Where I often see assumptions causing a lot of disharmony within relationships, all relationships, is when we just know how they are going to react. I hear it all the time: "Oh, I **know** they will say this," or "I **know** they will not take it so well." The reality is we absolutely do NOT know ahead of time how someone will react or respond. We *assume* that is how they will react based upon our history with them, only to find out often that is not the case.

Another treacherous road with assumptions is speculation. This is especially prevalent in the media today and is one of the most harmful things we can watch. I will delve more on this in *Chapter 9: Food for Thought ~ Mental Cleanse.*

What happens is that we often do not get the whole story. In fact, we rarely do. And definitely not if we only hear it from one person, one source, so we make assumptions based upon the information we do have. Then we take those assumptions and start thinking about what that can mean down the road. That's speculation. Speculation and assumptions are two peas in a pod. I always do my best to remove myself from speculation, either by pointing it out, or just leaving the conversation.

Why is speculation dangerous? It creates more assumptions, and here we go 'round the mulberry bush: assumption -> speculation -> more assumption -> more speculation. This will go on for as long as we let it and there will never be a valid answer, or peace. I call it future-tripping.

I implore you to practice ho'oponopono whenever you catch yourself future-tripping or speculating. Practice it as soon as you hear the first "What if," "It could ...," or "Maybe this will happen," and start repeating ho'oponopono over and over.

> I love you
> I am sorry
> Please forgive me
> Thank you

Saying ho'oponopono a few times will stop the speculation and bring you back to the moment, where life is really happening. The same thing applies when you start going back to the past. As soon as you hear, "I should have ...," start saying ho'oponopono and bring yourself back to the present moment.

The danger of living in the past or the future, aside from missing life today, is that we create it! Remember *Chapter 5: Come to Me ~ Calling and Feeding*, or the Law of Attraction? Whenever we are thinking or imagining the past or the future, we are creating feelings about each of those within ourselves. We are then sending those feelings out (feeding) to the Universe calling (asking) for more of the same, and the Universe always responds in like.

So that we are not making any assumptions, let's talk a bit about speculation and visualization. Some might ask, "What is the difference between speculation and visualization? It is often recommended to visualize the future we want. Is that not also speculation?"

Visualization is forming or imagining a mental image of something.

Speculation is forming a theory or idea of something without firm evidence.

When we speculate, we automatically visualize the scenario we are questioning. We heard a rumor, for example, and we start to form our theory or idea of whether it is true or not. Most of the time, the very fact that we heard it makes it seem true, at least until we hear something different. Or better yet, understand that hearing a rumor places us in the assumption space, yeah? We hear it and we assume it to be true, then we start to speculate on whether it really is true. Part of the speculation is visualizing the parties involved to determine from what we know about them if this could be true.

Visualizing is seeing what we think we want ahead of time, while speculation is guessing (assuming) the outcome of what is to come. Both are future-tripping, looking into the future; however, one is opening up possibilities while the other is establishing an outcome. Both of which may or may not come to pass, depending upon how uch time and effort we place on either one.

The main point about speculation is that it pretty much always involves assumption. When we catch ourselves going down that path, especially with others, as it is very contagious and can go on for hours if we let it, start repeating ho'oponopono over and over. This will break the cycle of the speculation and making assumptions and we can then investigate it further if need be. How did I create this for myself and why? Or we can just let it go completely, understanding it is not worth the time and energy to continue.

As for visualization? Keep doing it, just make sure you stay with ho'oponopono as you do and pay attention to any doubt! Whenever doubt pops up, immediately start saying ho'oponopono and get it out of your mind. As it has been said that a mustard seed of faith can move mountains, also know that a mustard seed of doubt may negate the desire to move mountains.

The fourth agreement is:

Always do your best.

This, in my opinion, is the easiest of the four agreements because we are all already doing the best we can. If we had known better, we would have done better. There is often an argument with that statement, and it is usually pointed at someone else, as in, "They could have done a better job." What is that, but judgment. Easy to say, but how do we know what state that person was in at the time they did what they did?

This is a good place to mention being kind to yourself. Always. We often tell ourselves, "I could have done a better job," and then start beating ourselves up, yeah? Let go of that understanding. At the time, we did the best we could. There are so many things to take into consideration with this. How we were feeling at the time, what else was going on in our lives, why we agreed to do whatever it was in question, etc.

Where this can become touchy is if we are doing something we have done before, and it maybe did not turn out as well as it did the previous time. So, we judge ourselves, often way before anyone else judges us. Again, we beat ourselves up. "I can do better than this." Then our old programming kicks in and we are off and running down the rabbit hole of guilt and shame. Ugh! Why do we continue to do this to ourselves? Because we do not know better. It is what we have been taught, programmed if you will, and for most of us, it is all we know. Why? Because that is the way it has always been done.

So again — understand that at any given time we are all doing the best we can. If anyone else says differently, remember that all judgment is self-judgment and here again, we ask ourselves, "Why am I taking this personally? Is this something that would be good for me to look into?" If not, then realize it is projection.

This is a good time to bring in the old adage, "Put the shoe on the other foot." Trade places with the other person. Put yourself in their shoes and see how it might feel. To reiterate, every moment is different. We see things differently, we feel things differently, and just because we may have been "at the top of our game" last time, this time we may have more external stressors. We may not have felt as good physically. Suffice to say there are a million and one possibilities as to why it was different, even though we were doing the same thing. Again, be kind to yourself.

A caveat: Do not use this agreement as a cop-out for doing your best. Please do not use the "everyone is doing the best they can at any given time" as an excuse to be lazy. And this is where the first agreement may come back into play. Be impeccable with your word. That means to self as well as anyone else, yeah? So, ask yourself, "Did I do the best I could?" If you answer, "No," then why not? What are you comparing it to? The past? Someone else's work? Now come back to the intricacies of the moment – what was different this time compared to last time?

Last time: I was in a committed, loving relationship.

This time: We broke up a few weeks ago.

Last time: I did not need the money.

This time: I am scrambling to make ends meet. I had to do it for the money.

Does it make sense that when things change in our lives, it changes what is our "best" in a given moment? Consider the differences. When we are in a committed, loving relationship, we have more energy, we are happier in general, and we are on top of the world, so it is easier to do better.

Contrast that with just breaking up with a loved one. That can be devastating for many. Why? (See Chapter 10: How Do You Relate? ~ Relationships.) I do not think we need to go into the "why" here, as most everyone knows what it is like to endure the loss of a relationship. Sadness, dismay, anger, frustration, and pretty much all the lower-vibrational feelings come to the surface, so we are far from being at the top of our game. As a result, our best is not ever going to be what it was when we were at the top of our game. However, that is not to say we did not do the best we could at the time.

It is often a similar situation with money. When we have plenty, we act more from inspiration, and when we are short on money, we tend to act from a place of desperation, yeah? We make different decisions based upon whether we are desperate or inspired.

A diligent ho'oponopono practice will help us better act from inspiration rather than from desperation.

So *Always Do Your Best* is not as hard as it may first appear. Remember, we are all always doing the best we can with what we have. When we say, "I could have done better," give yourself a break, understand how it could be better, and come into gratitude for the lessons learned. Be kind to yourself. If you could have done better, you would have. Remember to consider the circumstances before you judge yourself too harshly.

Remember, too, we often do not know what better is until after the fact.

Chapter 9 – Food for Thought

Mental Cleanse
What Are You Feeding Your Mind?

"a healthy outside starts from the inside."
-Robert Urich

We all spend a lot of time and money on our physical bodies. Yet we so often take our mental health for granted, not really ever giving it a second thought unless something happens to push us there. However, in the same way that we pay so much attention to the kinds of foods we put into our bodies, it behooves us to do the same with what we are allowing into our conscious and unconscious minds.

It has been said that we take in billions of bits of information every second, but our conscious minds can only interpret around 2,000 bits per second. However, our unconscious minds take in all of it! So, even though we may not be consciously aware of what we are receiving, it is coming in. Therefore, it is so important to not fall asleep watching television or have it playing in the background – regardless of what is on. Because even though we fall asleep, or are busy doing something else and no longer hear the television, our unconscious mind hears all of it and it is actually reinforcing those neurons in our brains – remember neuroplasticity? The brain responds to all input.

Albeit at a subtle level, it is still within you now and is very difficult to clean and clear because you do not realize you are remembering. Have you ever heard something familiar, but you cannot remember where you heard it? Most likely when you had a radio or television on in the background, not even knowing that you had heard it.

When you are in the store purchasing toothpaste, for example. Yes, we all have our favorite toothpaste, but ask yourself why you chose that particular brand. And not just toothpaste. If you are looking at a variety of similar items – the only difference being the brand, why do you choose one brand over another? Do you do it from a recommendation from a friend or relative, or do you suddenly remember a commercial on television? Or.... You are not sure where you heard about it, but you do remember hearing that brand name before. Somewhere. That is an indication that you may have had the television or radio on in the background and not really paying attention, but because our unconscious mind hears everything, it is a now a memory. Why do the same commercials get played over and over again? Because their makers understand neuroplasticity; practice, practice, practice; repeat, repeat, repeat. The more we hear something the stronger it becomes in our brains.

I encourage doing a mental cleanse. I did a 30 day, no television, no radio, no news. Yes, it was really hard at first, but got much easier very quickly. As a result, I have not owned a television for probably close to ten years. I am not suggesting you jump right into that kind of cleanse – but at least consider it. Take a look online – there are a number of different mental cleanses.

I think the most important thing to take away from this chapter is to start being more mindful of what you are allowing into your consciousness. As we become more mindful of that, we become much more selective. The more we practice ho'oponopono, the easier it becomes to be selective and change what we allow into our consciousness.

Have fun with it – try it out for a day, a week, or an afternoon; whatever is most comfortable for you – remembering that stretching our comfort zone is how we grow the most and the quickest.

At the very least, consider watching television with a more discerning eye, and pay more attention to how you feel when watching. When you notice uncomfortable feelings, say ho'oponopono a few times.

Chapter 10 – How Do You Relate?

Relationships
Self, Lovers, and Everyone Else

"If you're not comfortable enough with yourself or with your own truth when entering a relationship, then you're not ready for that relationship."

– Steve Maraboli

Relationships are simply how we relate to one another, and most importantly, Self. What kind of relationship do you have with yourself?

Are you trustworthy? Honest? How is your integrity? Do you enjoy being alone or do you need to have someone else around as much as possible? Do you ever feel lonely, even if you are in a relationship? Do you take good care of yourself, eat right, exercise, drink plenty of water, etc.? In short, do you love yourself? Unconditionally? Or do you beat yourself up with negative self-talk?
How well do you know yourself?

I do not remember where I heard this, but I took it to heart and have found it to be absolutely true!

"You can only know yourself as much as you are willing to allow others to know you."

What does that mean? It means the more we share our feelings, our experiences, with others, the better we can know ourselves.

Do you have any secrets? You know, the ones that are going to your grave with you. Yeah, the ones that would surely push everyone away from you if they knew. Those are the ones that prevent you from truly knowing who you are and why you are here!

I've had one of those. Let me reiterate HAD. Yes, I carried it for years.

For over thirty years, I suppressed it, and over time I thought less and less about it. However, it was still in my unconscious, and under certain circumstances, it would be triggered and come up. Then I would just shove it back down. What would people think of me? That I was such a wimp? That I should have been able to get out of the situation?

Here is the key. Once I told someone, and they didn't say any of the above, I realized that it was nowhere near as bad as I had made it out to be in my mind and imagination. THAT, my friends, is our biggest block to our own freedom from the bondage of self. Our imagination!

Think about it. Whenever you have been afraid of something, or dreaded something coming up, once you walked through it, how many times did you think, "Well that was not as bad as I thought it was going to be." Yeah? Have you ever experienced that?

Whenever we think about those memories that we are taking to our graves, repeat ho'oponopono a few times. In time, the hurt and fear will dissipate, and we will find that we are better able to talk about them. We love ourselves, apologize to ourselves, forgive ourselves, and find gratitude for the experience and the lessons learned.

I love you
I am sorry
Please forgive me
Thank you

The combination of the Four Agreements and ho'oponopono is the most powerful tool I have come across in forty-plus years of seeking!

Remember *Chapter 4: From the Top Down ~ Neuroplasticity.* The more we say ho'oponopono, the stronger love, humility, compassion, and gratitude become part of our brain and our consciousness.

When we come to fully love ourselves unconditionally, it is easy to be transparent, to let others know the real us, the authentic us. The more we disclose to others, the better we know ourselves, and the better we know ourselves, the freer we become.

The secret to a long-term relationship is to want, not need the other.

When we want to be with someone, there are no expectations or assumptions. We just want to be together. When we *need* to be with someone, we are lacking in self-love, self-confidence, or self-esteem. Essentially, we are lacking in Self and we are looking to someone else to fill those voids. That will never work! It often seems to work, in the beginning. However, over time it often slides into co-dependence and heartbreak.

I like what Paul Williams says in *Das Energi*:

"Don't seek beauty
Find beauty"

If we are looking for it, we do not have it. To find it, we must have it already. Within.

In healthy, long-term relationships, each person already has enough self-love that no matter what happens, they know they will be okay. Remember, when we get pono, at one with everyone and everything, and live pono, i.e., practice that oneness every day, we find ourselves in unconditional love for self. We know that we are always doing the best we can at any given moment. When we have unconditional love for self, it is much easier to have it for others. For everything.

When each person has self-love, then the relationship is simply a matter of wanting to be together because we enjoy each other's company and energy. Some would say "We vibe!" The reason this works so well is that neither party NEEDS anything from the other to help themselves feel better. Each person is already complete within themselves. That is not to say we still cannot learn from each other. In fact, in a healthy relationship, that is what makes the partnership stronger.

When we are okay with ourselves, we tend to attract a partner who helps us continue to grow and be the best we can be. Funny thing is, we tend to grow the most when we get our buttons pushed, or when we get triggered. I can speak from experience, that it is indeed a most beautiful experience to have a button get pushed or a trigger get tripped.

It is usually unintentional, but when it happens, we typically react and project our feelings on to our partner. In a healthy relationship, the partner understands this and does not react in kind. Rather, they will say ho'oponopono a couple of times and remind the other person that whatever they are mad, upset or embarrassed about is theirs.

It is obviously uncomfortable. However, If you ask, "Would you like to work on that issue and heal it?" the other person usually relaxes immediately. The two then begin a discussion using ho'oponopono as a foundation and ask the question, "Why did you take that personally? It was not aimed at you."

A conversation begins and because both parties already have healthy limits, it tends to be a much more objective discussion, and the healing usually happens instantaneously.

The same is true in all our relationships: friends, co-workers, family members, etc. When we have that love of and for self, we are better able to stand in our truth. As scary as that seems sometimes, speaking truth may be hard to hear for some, but it still generates respect.

When we are able to come together and heal ourselves within the relationship, the relationship flourishes. When we are healing ourselves separately, together, we soon find that the relationship becomes stronger and closer.

That is the easy way – when two are already strong enough within themselves to simply want to share their life with someone else.

However, as much as I would rather not say it, that does not seem to be the norm. There seems to be a lot of struggle and strife going on in relationships. And maybe more so in the longer term ones.

They all typically start out good, but over time something changes, what happens? How do relationships end up going down this path? There are a multitude of reasons, but the two most common I have experienced are the fading of communication and intimacy, or these two were never really there in the first place.Let us take a look at intimacy first, as this seems to be one of the key culprits for why a lot of relationships do not last or "stand the test of time."

Intimacy is most commonly associated with sex, yeah? If you ask random people what it means to be intimate, most of them will allude to sex, or at least to physical contact. While this is certainly true, intimacy is much bigger than just snuggling.

Intimacy is about being our true, real, authentic Selves. All the time. What does that mean, true, real, authentic? It means we no longer live our lives according to what we believe others think is best for

> "People think that intimacy is about sex. But intimacy is about truth. When you realize you can tell someone your truth, when you can show yourself to them, when you stand in front of them and their response is "you're safe with me" –that's intimacy."
>
> *Taylor Jenkins Reia*

us. It means we reach a place of self-love that no person can take away. It means we reach a place in our lives where what other people think of us is none of our business. Not that we do not care, rather, we no longer let their beliefs define our life. We live from our hearts instead of our ego. We live IN love, not FOR love.

It means we know our own truth, understanding that it may not match with anyone else's truth, but it is ours and we own it and love it and live it to the best of our ability. When we live this way, we can be nothing but real and authentic.

When we reach this unconditional self-love, intimacy becomes automatic. We are comfortable in our vulnerabilities. As it says in the meme, when we can show all of ourselves to another without fear of judgment, that is an intimate place. Yeah?

Why is there so much struggle with intimacy in relationships, especially in romantic relationships?

Mostly because sex comes into the relationship too early and the feelings associated with that get confused for intimacy, and more often than not, love. Then the confusion begins. Unbeknownst to either party.

I bet you will agree that if you were to ask people, "Have you ever been intimate with someone," and the answer is yes, what is the automatic assumption? Yep – if they were intimate, they had sex. And that is not so far off-base because people relate intimacy to sexuality and will also confuse it with sensuality as well. Sensuality often leads to sexuality, but better to not make assumptions.

This is what we are taught and inundated with on an almost daily basis through advertising. Buy this product and you will be more attractive, more sensual, more ... It does not matter what the more is – it will never be enough because it is external. Intimacy is not for sale and cannot be purchased. It is strictly on the barter system. We must give, in order to get, and the more we give the more we receive.

Where have we heard that before? Oh yeah, *Chapter 1: First Things First ~ Aloha Spirit.* Now it is starting to all tie together. Aloha and ho'oponopono bring us to living from our hearts and when we live from our hearts, intimacy is a natural by-product of unconditional love.

As I reflect on this, I realize that all of my close friends are intimate relationships, and sex has nothing to do with any of them. We just love each other exactly as we are. Yes, some days we get mad at one another and have our little spats, but because of the intimacy, the safety of being able to be in our own truth, we are able to very quickly and easily become pono. When we return to oneness and love, we are able to just love each other where we are, without asking the other to change. And the other side of that is if one of us sees a behavior in another that is unbecoming of their true self, we call each other out on it and talk about what is going on inside. This is where the intimacy comes to shine – we care enough to make sure our friend is okay, always offering a safe place to talk about the untalkable. We ask each other the hard questions.

We remind each other that if someone "pushes our buttons" or "trips a trigger," it is really about ourselves, not about the other person. "What is it within you that is upset by their behavior?" They are just being who they are, and it is not about you. We are good at asking each other, "Why would you take that personally?" And then talk about it to better understand. That, my friends, is intimacy!

Love   (I love you)
Humility   (I am sorry)
Compassion   (Please forgive me)
Gratitude   (Thank you)

... is the cornerstone of aloha, unconditional love, and intimacy.

It takes time. And practice. Remembering our discussion on neuroplasticity, we know that the more we practice ho'oponopono, the more it becomes automatic and second nature until it becomes easier to be uncomfortable. Because no matter what, we know we are safe and can now heal whatever it is that is making us uncomfortable.

Okay, now that we are all on the same page with intimacy, at least for this discussion, we can begin to delve deeper into what happens in the longer term with relationships.

Usually, one person grows in a different direction than the other and at a different pace. There comes a time when a relationship no longer works and often it comes as a surprise, like it just happened overnight. While that may be possible, it is highly unlikely. It has been happening usually over a long period of time, anywhere from a couple of years to twenty-five or more years. In my experience, it happens more often in the longer-term relationships.

The questions arise, "What happened?" "How did this happen without me knowing it?" "Is he or she having an affair?" "How did I not see this coming?"

Often, an affair is the first thought that comes up. There must be someone else! Yet, in my experience, that has never been the case. Even though there may have been affairs, they are usually on the side of the one who is seemingly clueless: the irony.

So, what happens? How does a relationship get to this point seemingly without anyone knowing it? Typically, something happens in the relationship and communication starts to falter and wane. Then assumptions begin to take place, and communication becomes stressed. This is because the assumptions get voiced and are heard in a way that feels demeaning. The defenses go up and a spiral down the rabbit hole begins, slowly at first, but gains momentum as time and lack of communication continue.

Then the communication becomes so strained that it is essentially shut down completely except for day-to-day responsibilities. The feeling of "walking on eggshells" becomes dominant and both parties begin to separate. At some point, it becomes so uncomfortable that they decide to try to talk about it. However, not knowing how it started and not having tools like ho'oponopono or the Four Agreements handy, the discussion usually very quickly goes back to the blame game.

At some point in this process, many couples opt for some kind of counseling or therapy. In therapy, it often becomes clear that the relationship has devolved to one of co-dependence. What?! How did that happen? We were never co-dependent!

When the communication starts to shut down and we begin to put up our defenses, we become guarded with our feelings and begin to be careful not to say anything that might upset the other person.

While we are here, let us explore co-dependence a bit further because this is a huge destroyer of relationships.

In my opinion, perhaps the trickiest, most insidious thing about co-dependence is that by the time we figure out we are in it, it may be too late to do much about it. Yes, it can be overcome, and the relationship can be rebuilt; however, it takes a strong commitment and due diligence from BOTH parties. It took both to get here, so it'll take both to heal. And where is the first-place therapists or counselors go with it? Boundaries! "You gotta set boundaries!" Well, like what boundaries? Not knowing what boundaries, or how to set them, is the biggest reason they often do not work. We have no idea what boundaries to set and most of the time we think we are setting them in order to protect ourselves, however, it is more often an attempt at changing the other person's behavior.

And therein lies the biggest issue. For whom are we setting boundaries? As I mentioned, we may leave therapy thinking we are setting boundaries to protect ourselves often coming under the mistaken guise of respecting each other's boundaries. But when we really look at it, what are we doing our best to do? Are we saying that things no longer work for me, so if you want to get along with me you need to change your behavior? Does this sound familiar?

And it is a two-way street, yeah? If I am going to expect them to change their behavior, then it is only fair that they have the freedom to expect the same from me. The bottom line is that we are asking each other to change. The irony is that part of the reason it even got to this point is because we had already started changing in an attempt to please the other person, to make the other person happy.

Let me reiterate here that I have never heard a therapist or counselor suggest that we need to set boundaries to change another's behavior. But because we may be so deeply ingrained in the co-dependent lifestyle, we hear that if we set boundaries, the other person should abide by them. That is where the confusion comes into play. Often, not enough time is spent helping people understand that boundary-setting is about self and establishing a stronger sense of self.

The difficulty comes because we must have a certain amount of self-respect and self-worth to be able to set those kinds of boundaries in the first place. Otherwise, we are doing our best to live up to what someone else thinks are good boundaries for us. Sometimes that works when we do not know how to set our own boundaries. It gives us a place to start; however, understand that these kinds of boundaries are almost impossible to maintain over the long term. To set strong boundaries, we need to have some modicum of self-love or self-protection to be able to adhere to them.

Each one of us changes for ourselves. But because of our individual paradigms, we often do not know that, until we walk through a few relationships to figure it out. When we add to that the media and the programming that is going on, we are being reinforced with this type of lifestyle as the norm. We are inundated with, "You make me feel like _____!" (fill in the blank).

As long as we blame others for our feelings, we will never be able to grow and heal. Yes, there are moments of following a protocol that helps us to feel better momentarily, and "momentarily" can last a few days or even a few weeks. This is very evident with all the, Self-help workshops and retreats.

We go to them, regardless of whether they are for a weekend, a week, or longer, and are immersed in whatever teachings we are there to receive. Pretty much everything about those workshops is centered around that. So we learn how to be vulnerable and feel exposed, we learn how to thicken our skin, so to speak, and we learn different modalities to help calm ourselves down. And lo and behold, they all work! Amazing! I feel so much better, so much stronger.

Until we get back home. We can hang on to it for a few days. Some can hang on longer, and a few actually have life-changing results from attending workshops. Why does that happen? Why do we feel so strongly, so empowered, when we are at the event, but within a few days of being home we are right back in the same routine we were in before we went to the workshop? Some of these offer boundary-setting exercises, and we set boundaries and are unable to hold to them. What gives? Why could I do it there, but not at home?

Within the workshops, we are surrounded by peers who are there for essentially the same reason we are, so we are usually all supported by one another. We all have the same or similar reasons for being there, so it is easy to support one another, especially because it is typically an intimate space and safe to explore our self.

We get home and we have literally no support – unless our partner attended as well. But even that is no guarantee.

I am a good example of why workshops do not work for most people. I have read countless self-help books and attended numerous workshops prior to the ones I attended with my partner at the time. But I was smarter than the average bear, so I thought. I had the idea that all I had to do was read the books and understand the exercises. Ha ha – I rarely ever did the exercises, thinking that knowing them was the same. No, it is not! We must sow the fields if we want to reap a harvest! I would plant the seed, water occasionally, then at harvest time be disappointed because I got nothing. Ha! Lesson learned? If we want the benefits, we must do the work!

We go to workshops and learn new tools. These tools work really well while we are at the workshop, but when we get home and we need the tools, they do not work as well. Why not?

This is because in the workshops we were living them and they were a constant in our day, but not enough to become habit or routine. When we arrive home, the first few days we are pretty diligent in following our new routine, but there comes a time when we want to sleep in a little longer, or something happens, and we just do not seem to be able to find the time to practice. What the heck is going on? I was at that retreat for ten days and did yoga every morning at 7 a.m. Why was it so easy to do it there and now I cannot seem to fit it in?

A number of reasons. Likely the main reason is, again, the support. At the workshop, we are surrounded by people wanting and doing the same things, so it is easy to join in.

When we get home, we must first find a yoga class that fits our schedule and get to it, usually a drive. Or, we can practice at home, but that rarely happens. It takes a lot of discipline to do that. And then you add to that a family member saying something like, "It is okay to skip one day. I am going to be late if I wait for you to do your routine."

We succumb to that suggestion, even though it crosses a boundary we just set. But we do not want to make waves right now. I am still in my Zen state from the retreat, so yes, I guess it is okay this one time. And what typically happens the next day, or maybe a couple of days later? Yeah, same thing. Ugh! Then we lose our workshop momentum and very quickly things are back to the way they were. AND ... the co-dependence has even returned. Sacrificing our self for the benefit of another so as to not upset them? Does that sound about right? Disheartening, yeah? Very!

And then we see another workshop, similar to the last one, and we think, "This time it will be different." So, we go to the workshop or retreat for another week or ten days and the same thing happens. While we are there, we are doing fabulously and learning so much! But when we return home, it is only a matter of days before we fall back into the old routine. Ugh! It is not old if we are still doing it. And the same thing happens; the family member cannot understand why it is so important for us to meditate, or do yoga, or Qi Gong, or any of the exercises or practices we learned while away.

This is another place where communication begins to break down. Rather than do our best to explain something to someone who cannot comprehend what we are talking about, we remain silent and do our best to not make any waves. And we start to withdraw from the relationship more and more.

The other person does not see what is going on because they are just glad that everything seems to be going along smoothly, perhaps better than before. They begin to wonder if maybe there is something worthwhile to these retreats.

Rather than ask, they just assume everything is fine and then they hear the news that it is no longer working. They seem flabbergasted and in awe –

how could this be? Everything was going along just fine! What the hell?!

The person who has been going to workshops and retreats is actually assimilating all that was learned at the retreats and they are becoming okay with being alone. They also now have a modicum of peace and/or a way to get back to that pretty easily. When we are in a place of peace, we tend to have much more patience and tolerance.

Meanwhile, the other person is baffled by the suddenness of it all. "How did I not see this coming?" is often heard. The answer is simple. Not paying attention and a lot of assumptions. The thoughts come in, "Well, he or she is not complaining any more so everything must be alright," but they do not ask. This is where the third agreement is so important: Do not make assumptions. These are the kinds of assumptions that cause us to take things personally and it is back to walking on eggshells. What they fail to notice is the other person pulling away, not necessarily intentionally. They are often able to be with themselves more and do not need the constant attention or validation they used to require.

Because it happened gradually, they did not notice the changes until they were such that they could no longer be ignored. Things like, "She used to get upset about that, now not so much" or "He used to get so mad when he had to wait for me and now it does not seem to bother him so much." From here, they begin to scramble to figure out what is going on and usually the first thought is, "They must be having an affair." And they are correct! Kind of. There is an affair going on, but it is with the Self, not someone else.

And this is where the real self-empowerment begins. When we establish a relationship with ourselves, we become our own best friend. When this happens, we change, often in very subtle, but powerful ways, nonetheless.

For me, it was about growing a backbone. Being able to say, "No, that does not work for me." The partner may not know what to do with that. So many years of "Yes, dear" and taking the easy way out, i.e., just doing what is expected of us even though it was never mentioned as an expectation, no longer works.

When I started standing up for myself, standing strong in my new belief about my Self, my partner did not know how to react or respond to that. So, the natural defense, the guilt/shame trick, may be applied, only to find out that it no longer works, either. Now what!?

Sometimes they will begin reading some of the same books we did, or even getting something we have not read, and doing their best to catch up to us in our spiritual journey. And it rarely happens. Spiritual awakening, spiritual enlightenment, spiritual growth is not an overnight process; it takes years. Years of doing it one way, then another way, and finally finding that connecting point where we find something that really works for us which helps us come to that place of being fully self-empowered and fully self-actualized. The years spent hiding skeletons in our closet cannot be cleaned overnight, nor in a weekend. There is no fast-track to awareness. Sure, we can all have momentary spiritual awakenings, but they must be acted upon and practiced to become a part of us. So again, the likelihood of the other person "catching up" is highly unlikely.

Often what happens is we see them "trying" to take more interest in the same things. So, we hang on a little longer, hoping and wanting them to get it, only to find out within a short period of time that they are not so committed. When we expect someone else to do the work for us, it never works. We cannot carry another on their path. We can walk beside them, but we all must do our own work. And yes, we can do it together, separately, and bounce things off one another, to help each other, but we cannot do it for the other.

I am seeing more and more where some spouses see the change in the other, like what they are seeing, and want to know what they are doing. They then start practicing ho'oponopono for themselves, and lo and behold they can once again start to share some intimacy, some new common ground, and they can flourish and grow together.

Chapter 11 – Just Make It Go Away

Chronic Pain

Eradicate the Pain

"Wait! You are telling me that saying those four statements over and over can heal fibromyalgia? How is that possible? That does not even make sense!"
-Carissa Lovgren

Yes.

I have, over the years of practicing ho'oponopono and helping others learn it at the deepest levels, developed a process that we work through to find the cause of our ailments, such as the cause of fibromyalgia. Once we can clean and clear those memories, the cause, the ailment heals. Ho'oponopono works with the cause, not the symptom – the symptom only helps us get to the actual cause.

This does not mean that fibromyalgia is not real. It is a devastating physical illness. However, all illnesses are a mixture of the body, mind, and soul.

The process of practicing ho'oponopono at the deepest levels begins with a couple of key questions:

How did I create this for myself? And why?

Remember, ho'oponopono is always and only about, and directed to yourself. It's never ever about anyone or anything else. Since we are each 100-percent responsible for everything in our lives, we had a part in creating our pain, our discomfort, our dis-ease.

When we can accept that we created it for ourselves (whatever "it" is), love ourselves, apologize for creating it, forgive ourselves for doing so, and find the gratitude in the lessons learned, then we begin the healing process.

Sometimes the healing is instantaneous, as in my lower back pain. Once I forgave myself for creating it, it went away in that instant. However, some ailments, like fibromyalgia, have so many components, it can take some time to get to the cause. See the rest of the story in Fibromyalgia Case Study 1 in the Appendix.

People do best when both the physical AND psychological components of illness are addressed. Chronic pain is becoming more and more widespread. Depending upon which agency you prefer, statistics range from 50 million to 100 million Americans. What exactly is chronic pain? The most common definition is:

> *"... pain that lasts longer than several months without showing signs of decreasing."*

Well, that is pretty vague, yeah? Which makes sense when you take into consideration how they may have come up with that definition. Many, if not all the chronic pain syndromes, have no cure, so all treatment is essentially experimental.

So being told that we are not able to cure it, we do our best to "manage" it. How do we do that? Medication – usually opiates of some form or another. So, since we do not know how it started and we do not know how to cure it, we will just mask it and make you think it is not there. Here, take a pill. And a week later take two pills, and a week later, take four pills, and now we are addicted to painkillers. They are pain-masks and spirit-killers!

And when we get into treating fibromyalgia/CFS, CRPS, RDS, etc., we have multiple symptoms to treat. More often than not, these ailments have multiple components to them, including depression, anxiety/panic, PTSD, bipolar disorder, etc. So now we pile on more medication. And in these situations, many of the medications have side effects that require another medication to counteract the side effect. And the roller coaster ride begins. When does it stop? Medically, sometimes never.

It stops when we take responsibility for creating the condition within ourselves. Yeah, I know. I hear it all the time, "I was not responsible for the car crash" or "How could I have possibly been responsible for that?!" No, we are often not responsible for the situation or circumstance that caused the original pain. However, we are responsible for what we do with the feelings within ourselves regarding that situation. Let us take a look at chronic pain from a different perspective.

My work with ho'oponopono over the years has convinced me that for any physical pain or discomfort there is an emotional component, and when we heal the emotional aspect, the physical heals. Funny thing is, I have been reprimanded a few times for that statement. I always listen to those kinds of comments and I gave it a second thought, even though its truth was staring me in the face through multiple experiences.

And then I remembered something one of my most inspiring mentors said in his book, *Conquer Chronic Pain*. Dr. Peter Przekop, DO, Ph.D., defines chronic pain on Page 23:

> *"Chronic pain is any sensation with a negative context in the mind that is holding one from being able to heal."*

I love Dr. Przekop's work with chronic pain, and so wish he were still here with us. He is sorely missed. I never actually met him, but in following his work, I find it very interesting that he and I were essentially working toward the same end. I from an ancient, native, spiritual practice, and he from a scientific practice. We both had the same goal: to eradicate chronic pain without medication.

As another example of how science and spirituality are coming together, here are a couple more quotes from Dr. Przekop's book that are relevant to our discussion (*note underlining is mine*):

Page 13:
> *"I had also read a case report of a person, who, from birth was unable to experience pain – because of a condition that altered a sodium channel in the nervous system that is responsible for the perception of pain – and yet during the extreme stress of a loss of a loved one, this person developed a headache. <u>This meant that extreme stress was able to cause pain even though the person did not have the physiological capability to experience pain.</u>"*

Page 17:
> *"I found that people who are unable to cope with chronic stress, people who internalize emotions, <u>those who avoided feeling anything that they held inside had an increased tendency to become chronically ill.</u>"*

I know too many people who were told, "You will never walk again," who are out walking around – and even surfing! How to explain that?! It's a miracle! Well, yeah, that is why I say ho'oponopono is where miracles become expectations. Why do they walk again? Because they believed so strongly that they would, that they could, that it became so. AND! They are not in chronic pain nor taking any medication. Again, how is that possible? If we use the traditional definition of chronic pain:

> *"... pain that lasts longer than several months without showing signs of decreasing"*

... then it does not make sense because most of the people I know fit that definition; however, they never considered themselves having chronic pain. Yet, when we apply Dr. Przekop's definition, it makes perfect sense!

> *"Chronic pain is any sensation with a negative context in the mind that is holding one from being able to heal."*

They were able to let go of any negative context in the mind, and in so doing were able to heal completely.

I get so annoyed when I hear about doctors telling people they will never do whatever it is again! In essence, they are instilling that negative context in the patient's mind! Stop it!

Too many people are taking it to heart and believing it, and it does not have to be that way. Would it not be better to say something like, "It is going to be a long, difficult road before you may walk again." At least instill a little bit of hope. Sometimes that is all it takes to change a life. I know from working with suicide that a little bit of hope can save a life, and I see it changing lives all the time.

Here is another place ho'oponopono is so powerful. Ho'oponopono helps us to clean and clear those "negative contexts in the mind." That is the purpose of ho'oponopono, to clean and clear any thoughts, feelings, actions, or deeds that cause us discomfort or "negative contexts in the mind."

A doctor says, "You are never going to walk again."

I say to myself, "I love you, I am sorry, please forgive me, thank you. I love you, Jon (always to self). I am sorry that I placed myself in a position where I had to hear that. Please forgive me, thank you." And every time I hear those physician's words, I repeat these four lines. Remember, neuroplasticity shows us that when we practice something long enough and consistently enough, it actually changes the physiology of our brains.

When I say ho'oponopono more than I say "never", it is not long before the "never" just goes away completely. The next thing I know, I am walking with a friend saying, "I remember when the doctor told me I will never walk again."

Okay, that was an example of ho'oponopono for something specific. How does it apply to the non-specific chronic pain ailments, like:
- Fibromyalgia
- Chronic fatigue syndrome (CFS)

- Chronic regional pain syndrome (CRPS)
- Reflex sympathetic dystrophy (RSD)
- Migraine headaches
- Back pain (includes sciatica)
- Anxiety/panic disorders; agoraphobia

These are the most common in my experience, and all of them can be healed as a result of practicing ho'oponopono. My back pain and my friend Tammy's foot pain were healed instantly and overnight, respectively.

My daughter healed ten-plus years of fibromyalgia with ho'oponopono. Nothing else in her treatment regimen had changed except the addition of ho'oponopono. It took about three years to heal because there were so many components to her pain. See the Case Studies in the Appendix for the details, but in summary, she had to heal agoraphobia and anxiety/panic disorders before the fibromyalgia could be healed. The process is the same:

> I love you
> I am sorry
> Please forgive me
> Thank you

How did I create this for myself? And why?

The goal is to get to the root cause, to the earliest memory for which we can take responsibility. In my daughter Carissa's case, she actually went back to a few years before she was diagnosed with fibromyalgia. There were numerous traumatic events that all happened in a short period of time and there was never enough time to address and heal from each one before the next one happened. So there was an accumulation of *negative contexts in the mind,* and as it accumulated, it began interrupting normal nervous system functioning. Blocking the flow, you could say.

What happens is we have all these negative feelings that we were never able to fully express or not express at all. Everything is energy and this is true for feelings, which are expressed as emotions (energy in motion) and when the emotions (energy) are not expressed, they create blockages in our system and usually manifest as inflammation or pain.

How does the body process pain? First, what is pain?

> *Pain is a distressing feeling often caused by intense or damaging stimuli.* ~~Wikipedia

I like this definition because it opens the door for emotional pain as well as a physical distressing feeling. So just because we cannot see anything wrong with someone, does not mean they are not in pain. This is why the ailments listed above are often called "silent" because the person "looks" fine. Let us take a look at how pain is processed. Note this is simply an overview that we may better understand how all pain, physical and emotional, is processed and how it comes to be chronic. Emotional pain comes under many names: anxiety disorder, bipolar disorder, PTSD, etc. It does not typically show physically, but the person is still in pain. As it becomes chronic, it affects their lifestyle.

When we feel pain, it triggers our nociceptors, or pain receptors. Their main purpose is to determine damage to the body by transmitting neural signals to the spinal cord and brain.

A lot happens in the microsecond it takes for the injury to register in the brain. There are six different types of nociceptors: thermal, mechanical, chemical, silent, poly-modal, and mechano-thermal. These determine at the time of the injury what kind it is: hot, cold, sharp, muscle stretch, etc.

Key areas in your brain:

- Your cerebral cortex thinks about the pain and decides what to do.

- Your limbic system responds with emotion: anger, fear, frustration, or even relief.

- Your brainstem controls automatic functions like breathing and heart rate that can change in response to pain.

The brainstem can send a return signal to the site before the pain signal reaches the brain, depending upon which type of nociceptor sent the signal. For example, fire would cause the brainstem to send an immediate response, or reflex, to pull back.

Once the pain signal reaches the brain, it passes through the thalamus where it is split and sent to different areas of the brain for interpretation. Was it hot? Was it sharp? Was it a muscle or tendon pull?

The thalamus also sends signals to the limbic system, the emotional center of the brain. The limbic system then releases feelings and we often respond with a yell or by crying. The heart rate may increase and breathing may become more rapid. Our fight-or-flight response has been triggered.

And it does not stop there. There are many other factors that affect how we respond to pain. Our mood, past experiences (memories), stress, etc.

Once the signal reaches the brain, there are a multitude of interpretations happening simultaneously, such as smell, sight, sounds, and memory. Has this ever happened before, and if so, how did we handle it? Also, this experience is now stored in memory.

This explains why we can feel pain just by seeing something, smelling an odor, or hearing a sound. For example, I had second and third-degree burns on my hands and was in the hospital for a week because of that. They healed fine; however, for probably a couple of years after that, every time I saw a news story or article about someone who was burned, it would send chills throughout and I cringed, remembering how much pain I experienced. I did not actually have any pain, but I could remember the pain and felt an overwhelming sense of compassion for the victims. And even to this day, thirty-plus years later, if I smell a certain odor, it triggers that memory.

This brings us to chronic pain that is associated with the "invisible" conditions.

When we refer to the definitions of pain, I am using Dr. Przekop's definition as I believe it to be more accurate, especially regarding the "invisible" ailments.

> *"Chronic pain is any sensation with a negative context in the mind that is holding one from being able to heal."*
>
> ~~ *Dr. Peter Przekop*

From Wikipedia,"... *intense or damaging stimuli."* What does that mean exactly? There is no "exact" meaning, for "intense" is subjective and can only be determined by the person experiencing the stimuli. What may seem intense for one is not necessarily so for another.

And "... *damaging stimuli."* Again, subjective. Stimuli can be anything: something seen, heard, an odor, even the air. It all evokes feelings within us.

How we interpret them based upon our paradigms is what determines whether they are painful or not.

Someone growing up in an abusive household will have a multitude of stimuli to learn to deal with throughout their life. Remember, our unconscious minds absorb and remember everything, even though we cannot consciously comprehend all that entails. When we take this into consideration, it begins to make sense why some people are sensitive to certain environments and others are not. All it takes is a certain smell, or to see something, or hear something, to trigger a childhood memory. We typically do not recognize the memory, we simply feel the feeling associated with it. It is uncomfortable and we do not know why, so we tend to avoid places that we know will trigger those feelings.

Therefore, it is so adamantly expressed in Alcoholics Anonymous to stay out of bars in order to change people, places, and things. When we are doing our best to stop drinking, it is almost impossible if we continue to place ourselves in those same environments and situations.

Albert Einstein said it best:

> *"We cannot solve our problems with the same thinking we used when we created them."*

This is where ho'oponopono is again so powerful. When we feel those feelings, we are usually uncomfortable. We often do not know why; something just triggers our fight-or-flight response. Not in the sense of immediate, imminent danger, but the defenses go up.

We can use ho'oponopono to help us heal those feelings. We begin by saying it in the moment that we feel them and if the feelings come back, we continue saying ho'oponopono. Then later when we have a little more time, we can pursue how to heal those feelings.

Later, we say ho'oponopono about the situation and ask ourselves, "How did I create this for myself? And why?" "When was the last time I felt this way? Yesterday, a week ago, five years ago, early childhood?" This is essentially the process and there is a transcript of a phone session in Case Study 2 in the Appendix.

Perhaps the most important thing about ho'oponopono is that it teaches us that we are 100-percent responsible for everything in our lives. This being so, then we are creating our own chronic pain somehow and blaming it on an accident, a traumatic situation, or whatever it was that caused the original pain.

One thing I have seen over the past decade is that for all pain, there is an emotional component behind it, and when the emotional aspect is healed, the physical heals, sometimes instantly. See Case Studies in the Appendix for more details.

There is one more aspect of chronic pain that we only touched on, and that is medication. We will start with pain medication, specifically opioids.

There are three main types of opioids:
- Natural opiates – come from the plants morphine, codeine, and thebaine.
- Semi-synthetic/man-made opiates – created in a lab using natural opiates: hydromorphone, hydrocodone, oxycodone, OxyContin, and heroin.
- Fully synthetic/man-made opioids – completely manmade: fentanyl, pethidine, levorphanol, methadone, tramadol, and dextropropoxyphene.
-

The most common opioids for treatment of chronic pain are the semi-synthetic/man-made opiates, with oxycodone /OxyContin being the most popular and widely prescribed to the point that we have an opioid epidemic.

Without getting lost in detail, we just need to understand that the body makes opiates naturally, just not in the quantity necessary for severe or chronic pain. The medications bind to the opiate receptors because their chemical structure mimics a neurotransmitter. They fool the receptors, allowing them to lock on and activate the nerve cells. However, they do not do so in the same way as a natural neurotransmitter, which leads to abnormal signals being transmitted throughout the neural network.

The opioids target the pleasure center of the brain, known as the nucleus accumbens, where dopamine is released. Dopamine neurotransmitters are not the only way pleasure is transmitted. However, dopamine is the primary pleasure signal. The opiates work by tricking the brain to release more dopamine, thereby triggering the pleasure center. When the opiates are stopped, the brain cannot replicate the trickery so the want and desire for the medication becomes stronger. Then the more that the medication is used, the more the body gets used to it; tolerance is increased requiring more medication to achieve the same effect. This is essentially how dependence and addiction begin. We will look more into addiction in the next chapter.

Note that there are also numerous other medications prescribed for chronic pain, antidepressants being the most common, but also anti-anxiety, muscle relaxers, etc. They all essentially work the same way by tricking the brain into thinking it is getting what it needs to ease the discomfort. And the same cycle mentioned above begins and may end in dependence or addiction.

So how do we heal these "unhealable" ailments? It is pretty obvious that medication alone does not work. Lifestyle changes sometimes help, but in most cases, they are very difficult due to the inability to function fully.

Our Common Rule is a healthy body, mind, and soul. So, anything that takes away from that could be considered an anomaly. Considering there is no cause and no cure for the "invisible" diseases, what is the next logical conclusion? For me, I believe it to be a disconnect from our mind/soul. A spiritual malady, if you will.

This being so, then how do we restore that connection? We have the body/mind connection going, but something is missing; otherwise, it would not be an issue. I believe the missing piece is that connection with our soul, or spirit, or higher self, etc. So how do we rekindle and reestablish that connection?

We begin doing things that are good for the body/mind/soul balance, or harmony. The first, most effective way we help ourselves is learning to meditate and doing so at least once per day. This is one thing that truly fits "more is better." Meditation is one of the most difficult practices to establish, albeit one of the most powerful. Be that as it may, when we repeat ho'oponopono over and over, it helps to put us in a meditative state. So, the more we say ho'oponopono, the easier it becomes to meditate.

This is another place ho'oponopono is so helpful. Whenever you are feeling any discomfort, just start repeating the mantra over and over:

> I love you
> I am sorry
> Please forgive me
> Thank you

The order makes no difference. It is also commonly seen as:

> I am sorry
> Please forgive me
> Thank you
> I love you

Remembering neuroplasticity, no matter how we say it, the more we say it the more we are instilling love, humility, compassion, and gratitude into our consciousness, our body/ mind/soul.

The more we practice ho'oponopono, the more we begin to see subtle changes in our lives. For example, by repeating ho'oponopono a few times, we are able to put off taking pain medication for two more hours. As we continue doing this, we soon find that we are now taking less medication.

Diet is also a key ingredient to healing. Not going "on a diet" necessarily, but changing the usual diet. Opiates tend to create cravings for sweets, or a sweet-tooth, and we satisfy this with a lot of sugar. Refined sugar is probably the most damaging "food" we consume. When we take less medication, we start to realize we are having fewer cravings for sweets. When we do crave sweets, we begin to think about getting that satisfaction elsewhere, like fruits. The less medication we take, the healthier our diets become. We find that we begin to prefer natural over processed, and organic over non-organic. The best part is, it happens pretty much automatically. That is to say it is not a struggle and does not require the, "I should eat this instead of that." We just naturally are more attracted to healthier foods.

This is further testament to ho'oponopono working along with neuroplasticity. As we change the physiology of our brains, the neural pathways and connections also change, and the more we love ourselves, the easier it is to take care of ourselves.

I will go into more detail about alternative healing methods in the next chapter about addiction.

This chapter would not be complete without introducing the S.H.I.N.E. protocol, developed by Dr. Jacob Teitelbaum, M.D. Dr. Teitelbaum's integrated treatment protocol was recognized in a major pain journal as the "standard practice" for chronic muscle pain conditions and fibromyalgia. He is known internationally as the lead author of the groundbreaking "gold standard" research on effective treatment for chronic fatigue syndrome and fibromyalgia (CFS/ FMS).
I strongly encourage you to check out his website and his work at www.Vitality101.com.

What is the S.H.I.N.E. protocol?

S.H.I.N.E. identifies five key areas related to the body that, when addressed in combination, provide a blueprint for promoting optimal energy. Tending to these can help you maintain healthy energy levels when you are well and can help support recovery when dealing with CFS and fibromyalgia.

The five elements of the S.H.I.N.E. protocol:

Sleep: Get adequate sleep, preferably eight to nine hours a night. Sleep replenishes your body's energy and helps heal your muscles. Inadequate sleep will leave you exhausted and in pain. Because your sleep center isn't working in CFS/ FMS, aggressive sleep support is necessary.

Hormones: Hormonal deficiencies can contribute to fibromyalgia pain and chronic fatigue syndrome. Unfortunately, blood testing misses the large majority of people with hormonal deficiencies and most people with fibromyalgia should do a treatment trial with the thyroid. In addition, if you get irritable when hungry, adrenal support is needed. Most men with CFS/FMS find that their testosterone level is in the lowest 30 percent of the population. If a woman's fibromyalgia symptoms are worse around her menses, estrogen and progesterone support may be helpful.

Low blood pressure (hypotension) is also a major contributor to CFS/FMS. Called orthostatic intolerance, this occurs when gravity causes your blood to pool in your legs when you stand up, leaving you easily exhausted and brain fogged. Do a simple quiz to find out if you have orthostatic intolerance. (www.EnergyAnalysisProgram.com)

Immunity/Infections: Underlying viral, bacterial, bowel, sinus, and yeast infections are common and can be contributing causes of CFS/FMS, or even the result of it.

Nutrition: To maintain normal health and optimal energy levels, you need to make sure you get an optimal balance of nutrients, particularly as nutritional deficiencies can result from CFS/FMS. Vitamin B-12, magnesium, acetyl L-carnitine, glutathione, as well as your basic A, B, C, and D vitamins are especially vulnerable to depletion. The Energy Revitalization System vitamin powder (www.Endfatigue.com) can optimize nutritional support with one simple, low-cost drink.

Exercise: Exercise as you are able. After ten weeks on the first four steps above, you should be able to slowly increase your amount of exercise without being wiped out the next day. Don't overdo it trying to follow "normal" exercise recommendations, as doing too much can result in Post Exertional Malaise, a condition that can last for days that leaves you feeling as though you were hit by a truck. But by following the S.H.I.N.E. protocol, you should gradually begin to improve your exercise tolerance.

Note: I copied the above from Dr. Teitelbaum's website (www.Vitality101.com). I strongly encourage you to check out his work if you are enduring any of the "invisible" illnesses. He explains in his books the details of applying the S.H.I.N.E. protocol for best results.

Pain, chronic pain in particular, is very complex, yet unnecessary. My experience has shown me numerous times that chronic pain can be alleviated without medication. Dr. Przekop and Dr. Teitelbaum's research have also proven that most people can heal themselves of chronic pain.

Any single method described herein can help chronic pain; however, if we combine them in any way, it expedites the healing exponentially.

I strongly encourage you to also read:

Conquer Chronic Pain, An Innovative Mind~Body Approach, by Dr. Peter Przekop, DO, Ph.D.

The Fatigue and Fibromyalgia Solution and *Pain Free 1-2-3,* by Dr. Jacob Teitelbaum, M.D.

When we better understand why and how chronic pain works and where it originates, it is much easier to treat and heal it.

Completely!

Chapter 12 – Chasing the Dragon?

Addiction
Regain Control of Your Life

"All the suffering, stress, and addiction comes from not realizing you already are what you are looking for."
— Jon Kabat-Zinn

What is your addiction?

Nothing?

Ummm, what about your cell phone? Can you turn it completely off for ... a week? A day? How about an hour? If, and I know it is rare, you forget your phone, do you go back and get it? No matter how far you must go?

I see people start going through withdrawal symptoms, panic, anxiety, and short-temperedness when they misplace their phone. Interestingly enough, those are the same beginning symptoms that present when one is withdrawing from drugs or alcohol.

I just want to point out that addiction is much bigger than just drugs and alcohol. I guess one could argue the addiction / dependence aspect, but the bottom line is that it is looking outside of self to feel better inside, yeah?

I also want to delve into it a little deeper than most, to the point of understanding how and why addiction does not start with the drug, be it a street drug, a pharmaceutical drug, or alcohol. Addiction starts long before the substance is first taken.

What is addiction? How does it get started? Why is it so hard to stop? The answers to these questions all relate to the spiritual awareness of the self. I have been addicted to numerous things and it wasn't until recently that I totally understood addiction. At its simplest – it is looking for something outside of self to make the inside feel better. While that may seem to work – it does not offer much of a solution to the nature of addiction, and as a result, many do not break their addictions – not because they are weak, rather, because they are unaware.

Once we become aware of how and why the addiction started, we can begin to address it in a more positive aspect and garner a much gentler journey into sobriety.

To fully understand addiction, one must first take a little journey into quantum physics. Yeah, big words for a very simple concept. At its simplest, quantum physics is nothing more than the study of energy.

Energy is! It can never be created nor destroyed; always has been and always will be; has no end and no beginning, etc. Some call it God, some call it

Buddha, some call it Jesus Christ, some call it Great Spirit. It really does not matter what label one puts upon it – it is energy. Each label has its own variation of the energy; however, it is still energy.

Therefore, we are all energy and everything around us is energy: rocks, plants, gravel, trees, water, and air. As such, everything vibrates and is in motion. Some vibrate at a slower (lower) vibration than others. We humans vibrate at a much higher frequency than rocks, tables, chairs, etc.

I think everyone can agree that emotions are energy, energy in motion – or if you cannot agree they are energy, perhaps you can agree they generate energy.

Anger is a good example. It is difficult to sit still when angry. We can even feel the energy building within us. More often than not, we pace around, throw things, break things, or even kick something.

It is very difficult, if not impossible, to just SIT in anger. Yes, it can be done. However, more often than not, the anger just continues to build until it reaches a point of DOing something, i.e., exerting the energy. Even while just sitting, we are exerting energy. Have you ever walked into a room where people are having an argument? You can feel the energy in the room, right? Enough said.

So, understanding that emotion has energy or vibration, we can now begin to understand how addiction works. The last piece of the addiction puzzle is that the "negative" emotions, such as anger, fear, sadness, and melancholy, vibrate at lower levels than do the "positive" emotions like joy, happiness, and compassion. (See *Chapter 6: Our Driving Force ~ Feelings*.)

I believe it bears repeating that a person with an addiction is not weak, just unaware. As a matter of fact, all the people I know who have walked through addictions are actually very strong!

Remember: Addiction is a result of doing something, like shopping, eating, drinking, drugs, or alcohol, to help us feel better about ourselves. When we do anything that raises our emotional/feeling energy level, we "feel" better as a result. What is happening is that what we are doing actually masks our lower vibrational feelings. We "think" we feel better because we now are able to recognize the higher vibrational feelings.

This is critical to understand because it seems that our "drug" of choice gets us high. But in reality, it does not. It only masks our lower vibrations and we "think" it gets us high. Do you understand the difference?

This can also explain why there is such a small window of the "high." We can reach a certain state of ecstasy and feel better than ever before. Then we start "chasing the dragon." This means there comes a point when the same amount of whatever we are using to make us feel better is no longer enough. We find that we now must take twice as much to reach the same place of feeling better. Our tolerance begins to increase.

The worst part of it is we are rarely able to capture the initial feeling we got the first time we did it. But we remember the feeling so well, that we continue to keep trying. When one thing no longer works, we often try something different. When that no longer works, we start mixing. And there we go, down the spiral toward hopeless, helpless, depressed, and feeling powerless.

We take the next drink, eat the next donut, buy the next pair of shoes. Then one day, we find our feeling of ecstasy disappears. Only to be replaced with doubt, guilt, and remorse. Then we ask ourselves, "Why did I do this again? How did this happen? I was being so careful!?" And the addiction has taken root.

It IS possible to feel good all the time without any external substance or stimuli. It is pretty simple. Not necessarily easy, but indeed simple. Stop focusing on the negative emotions when they arise. Instead, work on understanding why these feelings arise and where they come from.

This is another place to practice ho'oponopono diligently. Every time a low-vibration feeling comes up, the ones that make you want to use something to change, start repeating ho'oponopono over and over as a mantra:

> I love you
> I am sorry
> Please forgive me
> Thank you

As you repeat the mantra, ask yourself, "How did I create this feeling for myself, and why?"

Usually, the feeling begins to subside as soon as we start saying the mantra. As we continue to repeat it, we find that we are better able to understand why the feeling came up in the first place. Usually, there is some modicum of feelings such as fear, worry, guilt, or shame. Whatever that feeling is, as long as we continue to repeat the mantra, the reason for that feeling will bubble up to the surface. Then we may better understand why it keeps happening, heal it, and be done with it once and for all. Note: this is not one-stop shopping; this is a process we will continue for, well, as long as we want to be at peace.

It used to take a lot to get me angry. But when I finally did get angry, it was very often way out of proportion to the situation that triggered it. Notice I said triggered it and not caused it?

No one and nothing can *cause* us to be angry. Rather, the anger is already inside of us and it is only triggered by something.

I could not get a grip on this until I worked on my trigger. For me, it was something that happened between my father and me when I was about nine years old. I was extremely angry, but could not do anything about it; I could not express it. I just had to swallow it.

Well, I swallowed it okay, but whenever I got angry after that, my degree of anger was way out of alignment with the situation. Whatever it was. It wasn't until I did some group work and some meditation, both guided and solo, that I understood I was not angry with the other person. I *thought* I was still angry with my father, but more importantly, I was angry with myself. Since he was not around and I could not express it to him anyway, it came out at the current event that triggered the anger.

This brings up a discussion of the Law of Attraction as well. Like attracts like. So, with anger being suppressed within me, it was easy for my lower vibrational psyche to latch on to fear, lack of self-worth, disdain, mistrust, and related feelings. In other words, my trapped anger attracted all the other emotions that vibrate at a similar frequency to anger. So, I was not happy most of the time, even though I could appear so.

This is why we so often find ourselves associating with the "wrong crowd." We all have similar feelings (or vibrations), and like attracts like.

The reason it is so hard to break out of these relationships is because of the constant, consistent reinforcement amongst each other. (Please see *Chapter 4: From the Top Down ~ Neuroplasticity.*) I know people who are so strong in their beliefs that they will likely never be able to resolve them. This was part of my daughter's path in healing fibromyalgia. She had a couple of friends who also have chronic conditions of some sort, and they would have lengthy conversations, talking about their aches and pains and general complaints. She would have these types of conversations a few times per week.

After explaining neuroplasticity, and her understanding of how that is reinforcing the disease, she took the suggestion to stop talking about any of the discomforts with those friends. Keep conversations away from any illness, and if you cannot do that, then take a break for at least a week or two.

She also stopped posting "Fibro Flare" posts online. Instead, she began posting about going to the gym every day (even for the tiny amount she could do in the beginning), and pictures of her new food choices. Soon, she was talking about fibromyalgia in the past tense. Now, it is no longer a part of her! YaY!

Granted, a lot more happened to cause her recovery. She and I discuss her full story in the fibromyalgia section at the end of the book.

The point I want to make here is how subtle and powerful simple things can be as far as rewiring our brains.

I found out at an early age (fifteen) that alcohol relieved my feelings. If I drank, I felt better. And since all I wanted to do was feel better, I drank. However, unaware of what was happening when I drank, I often did things that I may not have done otherwise. So, I added guilt to my plethora of destructive energy in motion (emotion).

While the drinking did, indeed, make me feel better most of the time, the hangovers were worse than the "high" I had when drinking. Therefore, the drinking was only temporary. AND destructive as well.

To clarify, the drinking itself was not so destructive, but the amount I had to drink became destructive. The first time I drank I only had approximately 1 ounce of vodka in a large Coke. But by the time I had been drinking a few years, 1 ounce of vodka or any other alcohol had no effect other than to tell my psyche that a couple more would make me feel better. And it progressed until it actually killed me and left me with a near-death experience. This resulted in a spiritual awakening, a realization that this was no way to live. That if I truly wanted to be happy, joyous, and free, I would have to give up anything that made me feel otherwise.

I had to learn to go within to feel better without.

Eliminate anything and everything that makes you weak, and embrace everything that makes you stronger.

My apologies for the digression, but I felt it important to share my personal experiences. Let's go back to the idea that the addiction starts long before we take that first, in my case, drink. But again, it could be anything that we find that makes us forget or change how we are feeling.

It was probably only a few years after I took my first drink before I was addicted, but I could not see that for another fifteen years. I reached a place where I made sure I had at least three beers to wake up to every morning, and I had to walk across the street to the bar that opened at 6 a.m. to get a couple of shots of whiskey just to stop the shakes. Ugh! How does it possibly get to that point?

Get yourself a cup-a-tea and settle in for the long read. Just kidding. I will use myself as an example, as experience is our best teacher, yeah? Also note that in my experience in working with people and their addictions, we all have a similar story.

So where did my addiction start? Some would say that the alcoholism was passed on to me from my Mother. However, I no longer agree with that. It actually started long before that. But that is a story for my next book.

I would say my addiction began when I was around seven years old. I went to bed one night, and everything was normal. I woke up the next morning, and no Mom. And no explanation that I can remember about where my mother was. The next thing I know, a lady came to stay with myself and my two younger sisters when my Dad was out of town. He was a pilot, so he was gone quite a bit. She took good care of us with meals and discipline. But of course, that's not the same as a Mother's love.

So, after seven years of loving and nurturing from my birth Mother, it was suddenly just ripped out from under me. I would say this is when my addiction was set in motion. Losing Mom like that created a huge void within me. It would take me many years to figure out that I could not fill it from anything outside of me. Ugh! And I tried pretty much everything! It cannot be done!

Fifty-some years later, I figured it out. I hope it does not take anyone else that long. What I believe happened, not *to* me, but *for* me, was that in the process of doing my best to fill that unfillable void, I began to lose confidence in myself. My self-esteem began to wane, and I had no one supporting me who was in my corner. Dad was gone a lot and was not the huggy/feely type anyway. His idea of praise was "Nice job, but wouldn't it have been better to ..." Kind of negates the "nice job," yeah?

So, looking for the love and compassion that I had earlier received from my Mother, I began people-pleasing. I did not know any other way of making friends. I only knew that if I did something nice for them, they included me. To a point.

In hindsight, I now know that people-pleasing turns manipulative pretty quickly. I would do something nice for someone without them asking. Then, if I needed something, I would remind them of that nice thing I did – that favor. So I learned manipulation through guilt trips. Ugh!

And that is only the tip of the iceberg. There is a lot more going on in our psyche in that people-pleasing state. It pretty much goes against all of the Four Agreements! First, when we do something nice for someone, we automatically set ourselves up with assumptions and expectations. Then, when an expectation does not get met, we take it personally. Then, we sometimes lay the guilt trip on and if that does not work, we begin building resentments. Granted, it is most often written off as small and insignificant. But they accumulate, and over time we find that we no longer like or want much to do with someone who disappoints us all the time. Meanwhile, we remain unaware that we ourselves created the disappointments.

Feeling sad and dejected, rejected by just about everyone we "think" we care about, we look for something. Anything that will help us feel better. Our insecurities become more prevalent, our self-esteem and self-confidence wane, and we find ourselves in that spiral down the lower vibrational feelings. Searching for anything that will help us feel better.

We begin to feel anxious, and depression starts to settle in. Some go to a doctor and end up with prescriptions, while some of us turn to alcohol or street drugs. Others turn to shopping, ice cream, sex, or television. To make matters worse, the media and big corporations seemingly are doing everything within their power to get us more addicted.

If we do not have the perfect body, perfect weight, perfect nails, perfect hair, or even a perfect beard, there is a product to make it perfect. Weight is one of the biggies. I did my best to find out how many different diets actually exist. I could not get an accurate count other than it is a sixty-billion-dollar industry!

That is a lot of money for something that never works! Diets, as sold, do not work. Sure, most people will follow them for a while, see results and think they are working. But the regimen gets old after a while and pretty soon the same patterns that caused weight gain return. Why? Because diets do not address the underlying issues of why we eat the way we do. It is a lifestyle change that is needed. While that can be done consciously and with rigorous discipline, it does not have to be so difficult.

I am on the opposite end of the weight spectrum. It is as hard for me to gain weight as it is for others to lose it. I even get asked if I have some kind of eating disorder. LoL. Yeah, I did not particularly like to eat. Notice I said, "did" not like to eat. I was one of those fast-food, take-in, rarely-cook-at-home kinds of people, and the person I was in my longest relationship with was the same.

When I moved to Hawai'i, it seemed everywhere I turned I was told I should be vegan. So I gave it a shot and ended up losing weight and being sick. Ugh.

I think now, in hindsight, it is more a matter of acclimating to that lifestyle. Our bodies are chemical factories, yeah? We transform energy (anger to love), and we convert food to energy to fuel our bodies and our minds. Pay attention to that – fuels our bodies AND our MINDS. I think what happened was that I made that change too abruptly. Because since I have been doing ho'oponopono around my diet, a bunch of things have begun to change.

I no longer eat at any of the fast-food places. I am cooking at home more. I used to say I hate kitchens, LoL. My deal is if you do the cooking, I will do the clean-up. I began saying ho'oponopono about why I hate kitchens so much, or why I do not like to cook. I started to understand that it was a bunch of little things. Mostly the time thing. I had it in my head that it did not make sense to spend an hour fixing something that was going to be gone in ten minutes, and another half-hour cleaning up. Couple that with "plan ahead" or "what's for dinner" at 8 o'clock in the morning?

What? How in the heck am I going to know what I will be hungry for nine hours from now!? I did not typically think about eating or food until I was hungry. Then it was "I am hungry now" and I'd pull in the fast-food place.

As I am saying ho'oponopono and better understanding why I do not like cooking, another thing that came up was that I do not have a clue how to cook anything. Yeah, I can fry or scramble eggs and some of the basics, but to put a meal together? I did not know what spices to have on hand. I did not want to take the time to look up recipes, only to find out I did not have the cookware I needed. And on and on. So, I learned about all the excuses I had built up over the years and began healing those beliefs and letting them go.

Here is how ho'oponopono works at the subtle level. Remember the aka cords? The energetic connections we all have when we meet someone?

The next thing I know, I am talking story with my friend Terry and she says, "I will teach you how to cook if you want to learn." Ummm, okay – yeah, I guess I do. I started going to her house once a week and she was showing me how to cook. Simply one of those "out of the blue" moments? Not really.

This is how we start to see ho'oponopono working in our lives. We begin to see many more of those moments, or some call them coincidences (LoL), while others call them synchronicities.

While all of those labels have some merit, what is really going on is simple Calling and Feeding (the Law of Attraction). As I heal those low-vibrational thoughts and energies around eating, letting them go and feeding, to the Universe, I am calling in solutions and they show up, often unexpectedly or seemingly out of the blue. Then I remember that I asked for this. YaY! Thank you!

As a result, I am beginning to eat better, and the thought comes that I do not want to gain weight by growing a bigger belly. It needs to be evenly distributed. Uh-oh, guess that means some kind of regular exercise. A new gym opened in Kona, so I decided I would give that a shot. I used to like going – until I did not.

I am talking story with another friend who is asking me about ho'oponopono in a relationship. I find out he is a trainer. Not just any trainer, but a triathlon trainer. Rick has been in seven Ironman triathlon races and plans to enter another this year.

Anyway, as we are talking story, he asks me if I want to trade ho'oponopono sessions for training sessions. I just started laughing. He asked me what I was laughing about, and I told him I had just had the thought in the past couple of days that I need to figure out some kind of basic training exercise regimen (again, Calling and Feeding or Law of Attraction). I now have a training regimen I practice at home.

Lifestyle changes are not typically overnighters. I am practicing and doing my best to stay on track, but I still have my moments. Remember neuroplasticity? It takes practice and repetition to rewire our brains.

The reason I say it is not difficult is that I have watched people go through diets and I saw the frustration of having to eat certain things, while not being able to eat other things, which of course, the person is usually addicted to at some level. Thereby making it more difficult to follow a regimen.

If you see a diet that includes "cheats," a cheat day or cheat treat, run the other way. As soon as we go on diets, we already know we are going to cheat, so we set ourselves up again with expectations, assumptions, and guilt. This usually leads to more of eating the wrong things.

The more we practice ho'oponopono, the more we learn to listen to and feel our bodies. Then we notice that our desires change over time, and the first thought about getting a snack is no longer the mini sugar donuts (that was one of my favorites that I rarely eat anymore).

Instead, the thought of something healthier, like pineapple, or an avocado, or mango, comes to mind.

Let's look at sodas (or pop, depending on where you live). Sprite Zero was my nemesis. I became addicted to that during my opiate addiction days. I found the carbonation settled my stomach better than anything else. Anyway, that was a tough one to give up. I do not want the aspartame, and as my diet started to change, that was another thing that just went by the wayside, almost more in hindsight. That's just to say it was not a huge effort to let go.

The funny thing is, I did not have to stop myself from buying it anymore, because it suddenly was no longer as available as it used to be. LoL – Calling and Feeding again? No idea, but likely. I know a couple of places that always have it and where I used to always buy two at a time, and now I rarely even think about it.

All that is to say I want to offer up some food for thought, as I call it, about addiction.

Addiction most often carries a negative connotation, yeah? Like someone who is addicted is weak. That is certainly a major consensus from people who do not understand drug and alcohol addiction, as well as many of the chronic illnesses mentioned in the previous chapter.

If you are serious about changing your life, embrace ho'oponopono, and as you work with it, repeat it a few times asking yourself, "What am I addicted to and why?"

In summary, addiction begins long before the actual use of a substance or harmful behavior. Similar to how alcohol is described in Alcoholics Anonymous, "... alcohol is but a symptom of the disease," I say that addiction is but a symptom of our dis-ease.

A good way to check is to ask yourself, "how would you feel if "whatever it is" suddenly gets removed?" Do you experience any of the lower vibrational feelings as a result of not having whatever it is that is not really good for you, but "makes you feel better"?

It bears repeating: Repeat ho'oponopono over and over and ask yourself, "Am I addicted to anything? If so, what and why?" I think you will be surprised at some of the answers that come up.

In finishing this chapter, I want to clarify that I am not advocating substituting ho'oponopono for a twelve-step program, or any other recovery program. Rather, I am encouraging that it be added to whatever other methods are being used.

Ho'oponopono is especially powerful in step four and five work within twelve-step programs. Step four is maybe the most powerful of the twelve steps if we use it to its fullest advantage. It is step four that guides us into learning about and knowing ourselves.

When we practice ho'oponopono while doing step four work, it makes it much more tolerable and easier to look at ourselves. And when we fully embrace ho'oponopono, we are then able to do step four more like a treasure hunt than an ordeal, because we understand that whatever secrets or bad things we have done in the past are now the things that are holding us back today from being the best person we can be.

We begin to embrace the uncomfortable, for we know it is showing us something that wants to be healed within us.

Ho'oponopono is also very helpful with all twelve steps, but even more so with steps four, eight, and ten. I want to reiterate: Ho'oponopono is always and only about self! Never about anyone or anything else. It teaches us to accept responsibility (not to be confused with blame) for all of our own thoughts, words, actions, and deeds.

When we say ho'oponopono, we are saying it to ourselves, to our higher conscious self, and to our creator, whatever that is for you. Remember *Chapter 4: From the Top Down ~ Neuroplasticity*? The more we say it, the stronger it becomes in our brain and changes our brain. This changes our thoughts, which changes our actions, etc.

I love you	(Love)
I am sorry	(Humility)
Please forgive me	(Compassion)
Thank you	(Gratitude)

Love, Humility, Compassion, and Gratitude. Are these not perhaps the four most important characteristics of the fourth step?

When we practice ho'oponopono as we work through the fourth step, we realize we are doing the work because we love ourselves and want to heal. To heal that which we once thought was unhealable.

As we continue through the step, when we come across uncomfortable memories, we apologize to ourselves for whatever it was we said or did that caused the guilt and/or shame. We forgive ourselves, remembering that we are all doing our best at any given time. If we had known better, we would have done better. And we let it go, once and for all.

Make a note to make amends, where necessary, in steps eight and nine. And finally, give thanks for the awareness, for the lessons learned from having gone through that experience. For it is, after all, part of what made us who we are today. We learn that we do not have to live in the past. Rather, we learn from it. And the more we practice ho'oponopono, the more we come to believe that all judgment is self-judgment.

One of the things that can keep us stuck in our addictions is when we feel judged by someone else. It is even more difficult if that judgment is from someone who says they love us but continues to throw our past in our faces. This is where ho'oponopono again helps.

If we are feeling bad because someone is judging us based upon our past, without seeing the progress or growth we have made, we practice ho'oponopono. Then we understand that whatever they are judging about our past is not really about us. Rather, it is something within themselves that wants to be healed.

Unless and until they can forgive that within themselves, which is causing the judgment, they will continue to see these things in just about everyone they encounter at an intimate level.

When we judge someone else, say ho'oponopono and ask, "What is it within me that wants to be healed?" Remember that all judgment is self-judgment, and most often presents as blame and projection. This will help you not take on others' stuff when you are feeling blamed.

Chapter 13 – What Is Blocking You?

Creativity

Liberate Your Creativity

"Make an empty space in any corner of your mind, and creativity will instantly fill it."

-Dee Hock

What does it mean to be creative?

Is it true that some people are more creative than others?

Why do we have creative spurts and they seem to come and go at random?

Is there a way to keep those creative moments alive?

Can we force creativity and make it happen any time we like?

For some, creativity seems to be ever-elusive, and some will say non-existent. Why is that? Is creativity something one can learn? Yes – and here is how we can learn to release our creativity any time we like.

When we understand what is going on within our bodies when the creative process is active and alive, we can then learn to re-create those moments and maintain our creativity for longer periods of time.

The first thing we can do is dispel the common myth: The left brain is realistic, analytical, practical, organized, and logical, and the right brain is creative, passionate, sensual, tasteful, colorful, vivid, and poetic. While the left-right-brain idea is mostly true, it does not stop there. The neuroscience of creativity shows us that there is a much bigger picture than just the two sides of the brain. Creativity does not involve a specific brain region or specific side of the brain,

> *"Instead, the entire creative process – from preparation to incubation to illumination to verification – consists of many interacting cognitive processes (both conscious and unconscious) and emotions. Depending on the stage of the creative process, and what you're actually attempting to create, different brain regions are recruited to handle the task."* ~~ *Scott Barry Kaufman*

It is important to understand that many different areas of the brain work together recruiting help from other areas of the brain. Understanding this, we can assume that just about everyone has the same creative ability as the next person.

And the best part of all this is that we can now learn to activate and maintain our creativity any time we like. It is a simple matter of understanding a few basic things about how our brain works with creativity.

The brain has three basic neural networks:

The Central Executive Network
... is active when something requires our full attention, such as when we are focused on solving a complex problem or concentrating on a lecture; something that places heavy demands on our working memory. Our neural pathways communicate between the outer regions of the prefrontal cortex and the back of the parietal lobe.

The Default Mode Network (also known as the Imagination Network)
... builds dynamic mental simulations based upon our past experiences and memories, when we are thinking about the future, and when we are imagining different perspectives and scenarios for the present. This network is also active when we are imagining what someone may be thinking. It involves areas deep inside the prefrontal cortex and the temporal lobe, as well as both inner and outer regions of the parietal cortex.

The Salience Network
... is always monitoring both external events as well as the internal stream of consciousness and hands

over control to whatever information is most prevalent to solving the challenge. The salience network is important for dynamic switching between the networks and consists of the dorsal anterior cingulate cortices (dACC) and the anterior insular (AI).

The neuroscience of creativity shows us that not only are the large-scale networks (left/right) active, but also recognizing that the different networks of the brain all communicate with each other and allow the most helpful networks to work together activating and deactivating specific areas as necessary during the different stages of creativity. Sometimes it is helpful for the networks to work together, while at other times, not so much.

Our creativity resides within and is always present. We just need to learn to tap into it when we want to, instead of waiting for it to show up – creativity is a flow – nothing more. If it is not flowing, what is blocking it? All we need to do is learn to clear those blocks and we may then tap into the flow.

Research shows that creative thinking involves making new connections between different regions of the brain, implying that we can make ourselves more creative by engaging our divergent thinking skills and deliberately exposing ourselves to new experiences and learning. And when we take neuroplasticity under consideration, we remember that the more we practice something, the more automatic it becomes until we no longer need to focus our full concentration on it; we trust that it will be there when we need it.

YaY! Now we know that our left-right sides are connected. How do we actualize the knowledge? How do we put it into practice?

The desire to better understand creativity and how it works came about because I have been working on this book and I was only doing so sporadically – waiting for the inspiration/ creativity to ignite. That was okay as far as it went because when it did strike, I was able to get more done; however, it did not last and I did not seem to be able to sustain it. What do I do when I come up against questions like this: "Can I spark and maintain creativity when I want?" I meditate. Often, the answers will come very quickly, and this was one of them. I got the thought, "Is there such a thing as the neuroscience of creativity?" A quick search confirmed that yes, indeed there is. And here we are. Okay, cool.
So now I know creativity is actually a whole-brain function, not just the right side. What happens is the executive network is in charge while I am writing this paragraph, at least up to this point as I basically know what I want to say. And now I am having a block – not sure where to go with it. At this point, I say ho'oponopono a few times: I love you, I am sorry, Please forgive me, Thank you.

Doing this relieves the focus from the executive network, allowing the default or imagination network to come to the foreground. This is where we get our ideas based upon our past experiences and where we imagine or visualize the future: our imagination.

As the executive network steps aside, the default network is freed up to allow new ideas and possibilities to come into our consciousness, and as they come in, the salient network is always active. Think of it as a traffic light, allowing some thoughts to flow through, while stopping others. When the executive network is at a red light, the default network thoughts are flowing through. Then when the executive network light turns green, the new thoughts slow down. The focus is then back on the executive network to concentrate and put the new thoughts together, to make sense of them, to finish the paragraph, the painting, etc.

Remember, the key ingredients of neuroplasticity and changing our brains are practice and repetition. The more we do something, the easier it gets. When I first started applying ho'oponopono to sparking and maintaining creativity, the first few times I was not sure if it was going to work, but understanding that it takes practice and repetition, I continued doing it, and sure enough, it was not very long and I began to realize it actually does work, at least for me. I have written more in the past three weeks than I have in the last year or maybe even eighteen months combined. How do I explain it? I think I just did. Suffice it to say that it works! At least it is working for me, and as it has been said, "What one person can do, another person can do."

Chapter 14 – 10 Minutes of Zen

Meditation

Get Pono

"Quiet the mind, and the soul will speak."

-Ma Jaya Sati Bhagavati

I wrote the following articles a number of years ago to help explain the importance of and value of meditation. It was a series of six articles: Who, What, Where, When, Why, and How.

Who:

It is my belief that everyone should meditate. Now normally I would not say "should," because that is akin to me imposing my beliefs on you. Not a good idea; however, in this instance, I don't see that as a selfish thing. Meditation is so good for everyone that I truly believe it should be a part of your everyday lifestyle.

Everyone I have spoken with who meditates on a regular basis talks about how well their life is going for them – no matter what circumstances they find themselves in. And in fact, those who meditate on a regular basis simply do not find themselves in any kind of negative circumstances.

Then there are those I speak with who meditate for a while, then drift away from it and always say, "I need to get back to it." And my answer for them is, "When would NOW be a good time to get back to it?" Not so remarkable when I ask them how their lives were going when they were practicing meditation on a regular basis, and they all always say their lives were better. Less stress – actually, no stress; less or no drama; everything just seemed to flow better. Kind of like pulling the oars in and letting themselves just be "in the flow."

Finally, there are those who are going to "Get around to it one of these days. I know I should do it, but I just can't seem to find the time." Again I say, "When would NOW be a good time to set a time? C'mon just set a time for tomorrow when you can take ten minutes for your Self." Sometimes they do, more often than not, they will "think about it." Oh yeah, and those of you who say, "I just don't know if I am doing it right. How do you know if you are doing it right?" My answer to that is, "There is no wrong way to meditate, you cannot **not** do it right!"

I recently spoke with a new friend on Facebook and we got around to talking about meditation (imagine that), and she mentioned how she should get back to it – she used to sit and gaze out the window at the fabulous view she has and write in her journal. She never considered that as meditation; however, I implore you to check out my *What Is Meditation?* article to see how I am redefining meditation. Once she realized that she was in that place of "bliss," in the moment, everything was just fine, in fact, nothing really mattered much but that moment, she understood that it was indeed meditative. Do you, like me, ever have those moments – some call it daydreaming or spacing out? I suggest you look at them as a form of meditation. Anyway, she came to realize that was indeed a meditative state and she is going to get back to it because it is so enjoyable. She also remembered her days seemed somehow a little less hectic when she did that in the mornings.

Therefore, based upon the above story, I suspect that if you are reading this, you likely are in a meditative state much more often than you realize, but you just haven't put the label on it yet.

I will likely add more to this chapter at a later date. In the meantime, if you have any thoughts about meditation that you would like to share with me, please send me a comment and let me know where you are with meditation. Are you practicing on a regular basis? Are you wanting to get started, but are not sure how?

Please read the rest of this series as well as my article *Our Three Minds*. I believe you will find it helpful to read an explanation of why meditation works as well as it does, and why meditation is so powerful.
Thank you for being you.

What:

What IS meditation? Where is the first place you turn when you are looking for a definition? Usually, *Merriam-Webster's* dictionary, so let's go ahead and start there.

Definition of MEDITATE
> intransitive verb
> 1: to engage in contemplation or reflection.
> 2: to engage in mental exercise (as concentration on one's breathing or repetition of a mantra) for the purpose of reaching a heightened level of spiritual awareness.

I mentioned earlier that I was going to redefine meditation; it is not so much redefining as it is clarifying Webster's definitions. There seems to be a general misnomer that to meditate has, up until now, always been reserved for the "Spiritually Enlightened"; there has always been the ideology that it requires a specific *way* that it should be done, like having to sit in a specific posture, breathe a certain way, hold your fingers and thumb in a circle, etc.

I say up until now because it is time to change that belief system for it is by the second definition that most people seem to get stuck as far as whether they are doing it right. "*... for the purpose of reaching a heightened level of spiritual awareness.*" What is that? It is different for different people and almost impossible to describe to fit everyone; therefore, how does one know if they are doing it right? Guess what? It truly does not matter. We get so hung up on labels and what other people think that we often cheat ourselves out of the best parts of life. Stop doing that. I do my best to operate from the premise that "what other people think of me is none of my business." And I must say it provides me with a modicum of freedom that wasn't there when I was making sure that everyone liked me. DOH!

However, if you go with the first definition, you very quickly realize that you have been in a state of meditation a large portion of your life already, in other words, contemplation, or thinking, and reflection – is that not remembering? Let's go ahead and throw pondering in there, since it fits so well. Speaking of pondering, interestingly enough, if you go to the other most common dictionary, Wikipedia, under meditation and to the Etymology and History, you will find that *meditate* comes from the Latin (imagine that – doesn't just about every word?) root *meditatum*, i.e., to ponder. My apologies, I am not going any further with definitions – you have the links, have at 'em.

Okay, enough already. The point is, have you ever been "lost in thought," that place where time just seemed to disappear, or more aptly, not matter so much? You know, not really thinking about anything in particular. Sometimes it is seen as daydreaming, or spacing out, but no matter what you call it, it is actually a form of meditation. So, do yourself a favor, take the mysticism out of meditation and allow yourself the freedom to meditate whenever you see fit. The more you do it, the easier it gets and the bigger the benefits.

Now then, you've given yourself permission to meditate whenever you want, right? Right! Good, because now I want to add one more thing.

I want to put it out there that meditation is also a communication tool. Once you understand that we cannot communicate with our Higher Self, or Super Conscious Mind except through our Unconscious or Subconscious Mind, then you realize how powerful meditation can be in manifesting whatever you desire and deserve, for it is through meditation that we make that connection within Our Three Minds.

Therefore, in the light of redefining meditation, I would like to add to the above definition:

3: to communicate with the Unconscious (or Subconscious) Self for the purpose of gaining insight into true purpose.

I would love to hear from you. If you have any comments, suggestions, ideas, or feedback, please go to my Contact Me page on getpop.com and leave me a message. I will respond to all messages at my earliest convenience.

Where:

Where should you meditate? Pretty much wherever your feet are planted. Actually, that is not as difficult as it first seems. When you consider that we now have a different idea about meditation, and whenever we are lost in our thoughts and in the moment, that is a form of meditation. Another thing to keep in mind ... meditation is not a judge in and of itself. In other words, it does not only work for good. You may also meditate, or be lost in thought, about negative stuff as well. This is why it is so important to stay conscious of your thoughts; the more you think about something, the more likely, and sooner, it will come to pass. So do yourself and the rest of us a favor, and start paying attention to your thoughts. If you start to ponder negative things, stop yourself as soon as you realize you are doing so and change the thoughts to something more positive – starting with I love you, I am sorry, Please forgive me, Thank you.

This reminds me of the story the old Sioux Indian Chief told his grandson:

> *"You see," said the old man, "this inner struggle is like two wolves fighting each other. One is evil, full of anger, envy, jealousy, sorrow, regret, greed, arrogance, self-pity, guilt, resentment, inferiority, lies, deceit, false pride, superiority, and ego."*

> *"The other one," he continued, poking the fire with a stick so that the fire crackled, sending the*

flames clawing at the night sky, "is good, full of joy, peace, love, hope, serenity, humility, kindness, benevolence, empathy, generosity, truth, compassion, and faith."

For a few minutes, his grandson pondered his grandfather's words and then asked, "So which wolf wins, grandfather?"
"Well," said the wise old chief, his lined face breaking into a wry smile, "The one you feed!"

This inner struggle happens in our Unconscious minds and both wolves are constantly waiting to be fed. So, please be more aware of which one you are feeding. Thank you.

Everyone I know who meditates at all does so with a positive mindset. Part of the purpose of meditation is to dispel any negativity and to practice feeding our Unconscious Mind with only positive, self-reinforcing thoughts. Our thoughts are the food of our successes or failures. What are you feeding your Self?

Where in your body does meditation work? All of it. You can use meditation to lower your blood pressure in a matter of minutes, if not seconds, so it works with your heart. Usually, when you meditate, you are doing some kind of breathing technique so it is working with the lungs. It is slowing the heart rate, bringing in more oxygen, relaxing the entire body, as well as releasing any toxins that are in the muscles – so all in all, meditation works with the entire body to bring it into balance, harmony, and alignment.

One of the main focuses of meditation is upon the third eye. (The third eye is located just above your nose between your eyes.) When we use our imagination to visualize whatever it is we want to focus on, the third eye becomes active – the third eye is akin to a movie projector projecting images on the screen of your mind, your Unconscious Mind. The Conscious Mind cannot remember; however, the Unconscious Mind remembers everything.

When:

Any time is a good time to meditate; at a minimum, meditate twice per day, although this is one case where more definitely IS better. The best times to meditate are in the morning upon awakening, at night before going to sleep, and if you can, at lunchtime or midday.

While it is better to wait until you are fully awake in the morning before doing your meditation so you don't fall back asleep, this is also the time when you are very receptive to receiving information. This is when we are in an "in-between" state of awareness or consciousness, and the most receptive. This time does not last very long; however, meditation can help you extend it.

Okay, now that you agree that morning is a good time to meditate, and you have even set your alarm ten minutes earlier so you can meditate – what should you meditate on, or about?

I believe that when first beginning to meditate, there is nothing better than Dr. Wayne Dyer's *Manifest Your Destiny* meditation. If you have not heard about it or read it, I highly recommend you do so at your earliest opportunity. In the meantime, simply understand that the sound of creation is "aaahhh." So when you do your morning meditation, until you find another one, just continue to repeat the "aaahhh" sound over and over while thinking about what it is you want to manifest. It should go like this: Take a deep breath into your core, your abdomen, and slowly exhale making the aaahhh sound. Do this for a minimum of ten minutes a day for fifteen days, and I believe by the end of the fifteen days you will be quite pleasantly surprised.

For the evening meditation, you may stay with Dr. Wayne Dyer's *Manifest Your Destiny* and simply do the "oms" for ten minutes or so before you go to sleep. Actually, it is totally okay and acceptable to repeat "oms" while you are lying down and if you fall asleep while doing so, all the better. Do it the same as in the morning: Take a deep breath into your abdomen and as you slowly exhale, say, "ooooommmmm."

As you are aware from *Chapter 3 ~ It Is All In The Mind ~ Our Three Minds,* then you already know whatever is your last thought before drifting off to sleep is what your Unconscious Mind works with all night long. So, when you say your "ooommms" while thinking about what you wanted to manifest in the morning, you are feeding your Unconscious Mind that desire, and it will work on manifesting it all night long. Now then, are you starting to see the advantage of doing this for a couple of weeks at a time?

To summarize the When of meditation – anytime is a good time, and more is better. Don't get hung up on process or procedure, and if you simply take a few deep breaths whenever you think about it, you will be in a meditative state more often. Practice simple meditations until you become comfortable with how it feels to be totally relaxed. Once you recognize this feeling, you can reach it anytime you desire. You will find that you suddenly have less drama in your life, fewer people cutting you off in traffic, fewer incidents at the checkout, etc. So in short, life will be calmer and you will seem to be "in the flow" more often than you are not. Keep meditating.

Why:

Why not? Just kidding. There is scientific data coming into light showing that meditation does indeed improve your health and well-being.

What those of us who have been meditating for a long time already know is that it slows your heart rate, oxygenates the body, reduces stress, sharpens mental focus, and helps you to gain power over your emotions. And perhaps, more than any oter reason, it is just so dang relaxing!

So, there you go, no more excuses – everyone who meditates says their days go better when they meditate, they feel better, have more clarity, more focus, pretty much more of everything that is good. So again, why not?

PLUS, we can use meditation to communicate with our Three Selves. I am pretty safe in saying that everyone is familiar with the idea that we all have an Unconscious or Subconscious Mind, right? If not, please notify me via my contact page at getpono.com. And so it is, everyone knows we have one, but almost no one knows how to access it or how to communicate with it; it seems we are at the mercy of our Unconscious Minds, does it not? I am here now to dispel the idea that we cannot communicate with our Unconscious Minds. We can, we just didn't know how. Now we do – see *Chapter 3 It Is All in the Mind ~ Our Three Minds* and check out the How page in this chapter for further clarification. Understanding how our three minds all interact helps immensely with opening these lines of communication.

Have you seen the movie, *The Secret*? And, now that you know the "Secret," you are still not manifesting the way you would like. Is that a fair statement? I thought so – I hear it all the time; phrases like, "The Secret is a bunch of _____!" Fill in the blank with any word that works for you, but in essence, it doesn't work! Well kind of, the truth is that *The Secret does* work — it *is* valid; the reason it does not *seem* to work is that we get in our own ways and don't even know it. Why? Because the key to *The Secret* lies within our Unconscious Minds and very few understand that, and if they do, they don't know how to change it.

That, my friends, is my goal of these pages: to help you understand how to communicate with your Self so that you can unleash *The Secret* and begin attracting the life you want. Oh, by the way, you are already doing that – attracting the life you want, that is. I know, it isn't the life you "*think*" you want, but it is, however, the life you want. Once you delve into your Unconscious Mind and become aware of your paradigm, you will begin to understand how that is so. Note that not everything you "uncover" are things you are going to like or love. However, once you start uncovering and becoming aware, you will no doubt have a multitude of "aha" moments, as in, "Oh, THAT's why that happened the way it did!"

Is it easy? No, of course not. Nothing of this magnitude is ever easy; however, it IS simple, and therein lies the beauty of it. All it really takes is practice. Once you know the basics of meditation, just continue to practice on a regular basis and you will find that it does indeed get easier; even to a point of being second nature; in other words, you just enter a meditative state whenever necessary without really even thinking about it.

It is difficult at first because our paradigm, our Unconscious Mind's programming, is still too cluttered. THAT is why THIS process is so important, because you will learn how to go in and unclutter your Unconscious Mind. Free it up to receive all the new information that you want to present to it. A note of caution: you are already doing that. Again, I point you to *Chapter 3 It Is All in the Mind ~ Our Three Minds*, where I go into more detail about this. In a nutshell, everything you "say" to yourself goes into the Unconscious Mind – it remembers EVERYthing! So, the next time you miss a putt on the golf course and mutter under your breath, or not under your breath, what does the Unconscious Mind hear? Yup – every word, but mostly whatever negative connotation you say.

How do I know this? Simple, I used to do it. I stopped doing it – and yes, it is hard, but all it takes is practice, and I went from a twelve handicap to a six in a couple of months. If you are a golfer, you know how hard that is. The same is true no matter what you are doing, sports, computing, even shopping. Think for a moment what came just before saying "... should have ..." with your Self-talk. Therein, Ladies and Gentlemen, is why you are not manifesting the way you *think* you should be. You are not worthy of it. I am not making that judgment, you are. Whenever you say something to your Self that includes, "should have," you are telling yourself that you made a mistake and you are less than, that you did it wrong, or that you could have done it better. Does that make sense? If not, or you have anything else to say about all this, please visit http://themagicwords.net and let me know.

So ... gee whiz, it sure took a long time to get here, huh? So why meditate? So you can, first, come to know yourself better. Actually ... make that simply come to know your Self! Because until you truly know yourself, you are just basically cruising through life on autopilot, living according to your programming, which was given to you when? Yes indeed, when you were a child. As I said, our Unconscious Mind remembers EVERYthing while our Conscious Mind is lucky to remember what we had for breakfast this morning, unless breakfast is a habit and we have the same thing every day.

So again, why meditate?

Why NOT?!

How:

You will find it is much easier than you may think.

First, you are likely already meditating in some form and have just never labeled it as meditation. At its simplest, have you ever just sat and pondered or just gazed into space thinking about nothing in particular? Some call it daydreaming; some say you are spaced out. Well, I propose to you that those moments are indeed meditative. The only difference is you did not set out to meditate – it just happened. Another scenario: Have you ever been so intent on something that everything else around you just seemed to disappear, and nothing mattered but what was right in front of you; you were completely "in the moment?" My point is that there are so many people who say they have never meditated and don't know how; however, again I say to you, these are meditative moments. This all being said, you now have a reference point as to what meditation feels like. It really is that simple. The only difference is that you did not set out to meditate, it just happened.

Now then, all that is left is to do it on purpose or with intent. The easiest way is to make sure you set aside some time. When you are first beginning to practice meditation, it doesn't matter how long, simply make sure you set aside some time when you will be totally alone with no external influences of any kind, no music, no television, no phones, no computer, etc. Make your meditation environment as quiet as possible.

I know it is difficult to do it for very long when you have never done this before, which is why I recommend setting aside only twenty minutes. If, for whatever reason, you cannot sit completely still for twenty minutes, then start with ten minutes – the important thing is to set aside the time for the specific purpose of sitting quietly. It is perfectly acceptable to set an alarm for however long you want to meditate so you do not have the tendency to "peek" at a clock – just sit until the alarm goes off.

Once you have set your space and time and are ready to begin, simply take a few slow, deep breaths. I recommend breathing in through your nose, holding it for a second and exhaling slowly through your mouth. With each breath, just allow yourself to relax.

Once you feel relaxed, simply say to yourself, "Please show me a good memory of my childhood." Actually saying it is best, but even if you just say it silently, that is a good start. Once you have said that, just sit quietly. Pay attention to how you feel, what you feel, and where in your body you feel it. The first few times you may not "get" anything, but stay with it and within a short time, you will start to remember something of your childhood that you haven't thought about in a long time. Once that memory comes in, just allow it to unfold. I would bet "dollars to donuts," as the saying goes, that once this happens, you will likely sit there longer than the ten or twenty minutes you allotted your Self.

Yes, there are a multitude of books, online resources, CDs, and DVDs that explain how to meditate. You are certainly free to pursue them and spend a lot of time figuring out the best way to learn to meditate. Please be careful that you do not spend all of your time "learning" and not meditating. That being said, I am not claiming that this is the best way to learn to meditate; rather, I believe it to be the simplest. My goal is to help people to learn and practice meditation. It matters not to me how you learn or how you meditate, just please do yourself and the rest of humanity a favor and practice meditation on a regular basis.

There are also probably as many breathing techniques, postures, and other varieties of meditation as there are people teaching them. I recommend that you delve into them if you are so inclined; however, please wait until you are comfortable just sitting quietly for at least a half-hour at a time – an hour would be better – but just be sure you are comfortable with being able to sit quietly before expanding on other ways to meditate.

Once you are comfortable sitting quietly for a period of time, then by all means, experiment to your heart's content. As I said, there are innumerable ways to meditate and a myriad of different meditations. For example, you may want to do a crystal or gemstone meditation, a candle meditation, listen to music, etc. And finally, once you are more comfortable sitting or lying quietly, you will find you can meditate "ON" something; for example, you may have a decision to make or a challenge that needs a solution. Meditation is a great way to arrive at the best answer or solution.

Conclusion

Actually? This is just the beginning! It is my hope and prayer that you at least get something from these words. I promise if you say the magic words:

> Love
> Humility
> Compassion
> Gratitude

...your life will change. The easiest way I have found to use these magic words is ho'oponopono,

> I love you
> I am sorry
> Please forgive me
> Thank you

Say the mantra all the time, over and over. Say it until it becomes automatic so when you find yourself not thinking of anything in particular, daydreaming, just start repeating it.

Stay present to how you feel and if you feel anything less than happiness or joy, repeat the mantra over and over until the feeling subsides. Remember, depending upon the circumstances, the feeling may come back right away in which case just start repeating it again. Soon you will realize the feelings are further apart and less intense. And it will not be long before they do not surface at all.

Say it before you walk into any meeting, before you make a phone call, especially if the meeting or call is with someone you may be at odds with.

Morrnah Simeona was asked in an interview, "How often should one say ho'oponopono?" Morrnah replied, "All the time!"

When I took her advice and started saying it all the time, my life began changing in the most profound ways.

As I said at the beginning of this conclusion – "This is just the beginning." I have two more books in process, one of which is a companion workbook to accompany this book.

The companion book will show you how to go the deepest levels of self. It is structured in such a way as to allow you to choose how deeply you want to explore.

Thank you so much for reading these words. In so doing, whether you realize it or not you have done a big part in releasing Love, Humility, Compassion, and Gratitude back to the Universe for all.

The more we do this, the more we heal at the All Souls level.

Pono – at one with everyone and everything!

Appendix I

In the Beginning Is the Word

We often underestimate the power of our words. I remember growing up and hearing,

> *"Be careful with your words, they are the one thing you can never take back."*

I want to focus on a few of the most common words that hold us back from being all we can be.

"Try", "Can't", "Should", and "Have to".

Try:

I always liked the definition of try: "Failing with dignity." I believe that to be an accurate metaphor. And of course, a discussion of try would not be complete without the quote from Yoda, "Do. Or do not. There is no try."

I decided to eliminate "try" from my vocabulary a few years ago. Cannot do it; however, I almost always catch myself and correct it immediately. When I catch myself saying "try," I immediately replace it with "do my best …"

It is difficult to see how this could make a difference, but I have noticed a big difference at work since I have stopped trying. I used to say I will try to get that report done by whatever date and was always scrambling at the end to get it done on time. When I began replacing try with do my best, "I will do my best to get it to you then," I now am always early or right on time – without having to scramble at the end.

Try also has a tendency to place us in a blaming state. "Well, I tried, but yada yada yada – excuses. Remember, when we live a ho'oponopono lifestyle, live pono, there are no more excuses.

I implore you to eliminate the word try from your vocabulary. No, it's not likely you will be able to eradicate it completely; however, catching and replacing it as soon as you say it does work very well.

And ... doing this will reinforce the fourth agreement: Always Do Your Best.

Try it out! LoL

Can't:

Can't is rarely ever true. We have been so programmed with it and it has become so commonplace that we do not even think about what we are saying.

Nine times out of ten, can't really means won't.

This applies more to our commitments than anything else.

Another thing I have done is to stop using contractions as much as possible. Two things happen when we do this.

We become more conscious of what we are saying. Can't is a contraction of cannot. I know it sounds weird, but if we start saying cannot instead of can't, we begin to realize that, lo and behold, we actually CAN do whatever we are saying it about – we just do not want to. And if we use can't, it sounds like it is beyond our control and we are not capable of doing it. Like something or someone is stopping us. Not true, most of the time.

When I catch myself saying cannot, I immediately ask myself if it is actually true, or if "will not" is a better answer. Will not is more accurate most of the time. It is quite rare that I cannot do something.

Should:

I would like to see the word should eliminated from the English language. LoL

Should is perhaps the greatest shame/guilt word there is. In my experience talking story with a lot of people, it is the most limiting word in their lives.

Most of us, when growing up, just wanted to make our parents proud of us. In order to do that, we learned that we should do certain things in a certain way. "That is just the way it has always been done." Remember the holiday dinner story?

More often than not, should is what someone else thinks is best for us. If we want to be successful, we should go to school, we should get good grades, we should go to college, we should get a good job, etc.

How often, when you are telling someone about an unpleasant situation that happened, do they say, "You should … do or say this." And how often do you say it to someone else when the tables are turned?

Be mindful of should. Do you say it thinking that you know better what is right for someone else? None of us know what is right for another person. Yes, we can suggest something based upon our own personal experiences; however, is it not better to say "could" rather than should? Again, should sounds like options are limited, whereas, could opens up options. Should insinuates no choice; could gives back choice.

Have to:

No! We GET to. Remember, ho'oponopono teaches us that we are each 100-percent responsible for everything in our lives.

When we say "… have to …," it insinuates that we do not have a choice. I hear it all the time and correct it to "get to." My friends often get annoyed and start to argue with me, but soon give in because they finally realize they cannot win that argument.

"I have to go to work."
"You GET to go to work."

"No, I have to!"

"No, you could choose to stay here and drink kava all afternoon. The consequences may not be so desirable, but it IS a choice, nonetheless."

"Oh yeah, huh."

I typically hear this the most from people who do not like their jobs. And I remind them that it is a choice to go to work and why would you make a choice to go somewhere where you will be unhappy or miserable? If we are going to make the choice to go to work, I would rather figure out a way to make it enjoyable than not. It places us in a state of gratitude – we can become grateful we have the job, understanding that it is likely not the last job we will ever have. Likely it is more of a stepping stone to the next phase.

Haha – reminds me of another thing I like to say that seems to annoy certain people. LoL

> *"If you are not doing what you love, love what you are doing and soon you will be doing what you love."*

Whenever you catch yourself saying "have to," rephrase it and say, "get to." Notice how it feels when you rephrase it.

Pay attention to all these words and replace them as often as you hear yourself say them or think them.

Try -> Do my best

Can't -> Won't (start using cannot and will not)

Have to -> Get to

Should -> Could

Feel the difference. I often say that ho'oponopono gives us conscious communication with our unconscious minds. The Language of Ho'oponopono, if you will. The vocabulary is our feelings!

Feel into the words above – the words on the left feel like we have no choice, whereas the words on the right give us choice.

Choice is empowering!

Appendix II

The 7 Laws of the Universe

When we understand these 7 basic Laws of the Universe, we may better understand the Law of Attraction – or as we spoke of earlier, Calling and Feeding. The Law of Attraction is essentially the culmination of the other 7 laws. When we understand the laws, we are better able to work within them as well as better understand why things happen the way and in the time they do.

1. Perpetual Transformation of Energy

Energy can never be created nor destroyed, it always has been and will be, it is constantly moving into and out of form.

This energy is limitless and inexhaustible, always changing, transforming. We are energy transformers. As the energy flows through us, our thoughts, feelings, and emotions are constantly changing the energy, so it is up to each of us to maintain a positive, loving energy flow.

2. Law of Vibration

Everything in the Universe has its own vibrational frequency, including all our thoughts, feelings, actions, and deeds. What we are thinking and feeling is sending out vibrations, and the Universe matches those vibrations.

The more we practice ho'oponopono, the more we are sending out love, humility, compassion, and gratitude frequencies and vibrations. And we find ourselves living pono – at one with everyone and everything.

3. Law of Relativity

Everything just is. Everything is made real by comparing it to something else. Good vs. bad, light vs. dark, hot vs. cold, etc.

Something is only good or bad if we compare it to something or someone else. Remember, not one of us is any better nor any worse than anyone else. Since the Universe is completely neutral, there really is no good or bad; there is, however, comfortable and uncomfortable.

4. Law of Polarity

Electricity (energy) has a positive and a negative charge. The earth has opposite poles (north/south); think opposites. Left/right, up/down, inside/outside, positive/negative, etc. We are in a dualistic Universe and as such, everything has an equal opposite. So how do we apply this law?

This law comes into play when we are experiencing something very "bad," because no matter how bad something is, there is an equal and opposite good side.

I used to remind myself, "If it is this bad for this long, the blessings on the other side will be phenomenal!" and it has always proven true. When something seems bad, start looking for the good in it. Most of the time we cannot see the good when we are sitting in the middle of bad, but the very act of looking for the good starts to raise us out of the bad feeling. We can transform our thoughts from hate to love, from fear to courage, by consciously raising our vibrations.

And the simplest way I have found to raise my vibrations is with ho'oponopono.

I love you, I am sorry, please forgive me, thank you. When feeling "bad," just repeat over and over and over again. Say it over and over until it becomes automatic.

5. Law of Rhythm

There is a rhythm to the Universe: sunrise, sunset, moon around the planet every twenty-eight days, four seasons. Watch the waves on the ocean; they come in sets, and when you tune into the rhythm, you can know when the next big wave is due.

Our heartbeat has a rhythm, and music has a rhythm. Understanding the law of rhythm shows us that the old adage "this too shall pass" is absolutely true. We sometimes must go to extremes on both sides to find out what the middle ground is, to know our rhythm.

Once we know our own rhythm, we can begin to stay within it. A diligent ho'oponopono practice helps us recognize when we are starting to go out of our rhythm and we learn to come back very quickly into it.

6. Law of Cause and Effect

For every cause there is an effect, a consequence, if you will. This is pretty easy to see in the physical world; however, it also operates in the spirit within each of us.

That being so, it behooves us to pay attention to our thoughts, words, actions, and deeds as they are causal.

Ho'oponopono teaches us to recognize the more subtle cause/effect scenarios. Our thoughts, words, actions, and deeds contribute to our feelings. Remember our feelings are "cat food," – always feeding the Universe calling for more of the same.

A friend I was talking story with a couple of years ago said she lived in the same house as her mom, and it seemed that every time she came in the front door, an argument started. Why? Because each one of them already has the argument played out a number of different ways in their own minds. And sure enough, an argument ensues.

I suggested she start saying ho'oponopono: I love you, I am sorry, please forgive me, thank you, on the way to the door before going in. She started doing so and was surprised, but the arguing stopped immediately. Why? A few reasons: it shuts down the negative "get ready for a battle" thought process, it brings us into the present moment instead of future-tripping about the encounter, and most importantly, it brings us to our hearts, and when we are living from our hearts, it brings us out of our low-vibration negative feelings and into the positive, love, joy, and peace feelings.

When she was saying ho'oponopono on the way into the house, she was sending out love, humility, compassion, and gratitude, asking for more of the same – remember, we always get what we ask for. So, when she walked in the house, she was of a loving vibration and her mom did not feel the negative, low-vibration energies she was expecting, so at first, she was a bit taken aback, but very quickly became responsive rather than reactive. They actually started having peaceful, more meaningful conversations.

7. Law of Gender

Gender is in everything. It is the masculine/feminine, the yin/ yang. Some feminine qualities are love, patience, intuition, and gentleness. The masculine are energy, self-reliance, logic, and intellect. We each have all the above. When we bring the feminine and masculine into balance, then we are complete.

This law also reminds us that all seeds (ideas, desires) have a gestation or incubation period. There was a time when we did not know it took nine months for a baby to be born, or when the first carrot seed, or any seed for that matter, was planted, how long it would take to germinate. We now know it takes about two to three weeks for a carrot seed to germinate. When we have a new idea or desire, we have no idea how long it will take to manifest. There are a lot of variables at play and any one of them not in alignment with the request can negate it.

If we get impatient, we may start to doubt or second-guess our idea. Remember: the same way a mustard seed of faith can move mountains, a mustard seed of doubt can stop them in their tracks.

If we begin to question our intuition or our logic or intellect, or start trying to make it happen faster, then it is a good time to practice ho'oponopono and bring ourselves back to love and gratitude.

Appendix III

The 7 Chakras

Think of our chakras as energy wheels. Each one has the characteristics listed below. The more we practice ho'oponopono, the more highly attuned we become of our feelings.

I am including these for reference only. There are a multitude of books about chakras so you may go as deeply into them as you like.

Chakra	1 - MULADHARA (Root)
Symbol	4 petaled Lotus
Color	Red
Location	Between genitals and anus
Principle	Physical Entity
Purpose	Links the individual with the physical world
Element	Earth
Gems	Agate, Bloodstone Garnet, Ruby, Smoky Quartz
Oils	Cedar, Clove, Cypress, Marjoram, Myrrh
Sense	Smell
Effect	Calms, dissolves tension
Aura	Etheric body
Body parts	Bones, teeth, nails, legs, arms, intestine, anus, prostate, blood, cell structure, adrenal gland
Massage direction female	Counter-clockwise
Massage direction male	Clockwise
Mantra	Lam
Tone	C
Zodiac and planets	Aries, Mars, Taurus, Scorpio, Capricorn, Saturn

Chakra	2 - SVADHISTHANA (Sacral)
Symbol	6 petaled Lotus
Color	Orange
Location	Slightly above genital area below navel
Principle	Reproduction of being
Purpose	Center for sexual energy, creativity, and pure emotions
Element	Water
Gems	Moonstone, Carnelian, Tourmaline
Oils	Sandalwood, Petitgrain, Ylang Ylang
Sense	Taste
Effect	Stimulates desire, rejuvenates
Aura	Emotional body
Body parts	Reproductive organs, kidney, bladder, pelvic area, sperm, all liquids and fluids of the body
Massage direction female	Clockwise
Massage direction male	Counter-clockwise
Mantra	Vam
Tone	D
Zodiac and planets	Cancer, Libra, Scorpio, Moon, Venus, Mars, Mercury

Chakra	3 - MANIPURA (Solar Plexus)
Symbol	10 petaled Lotus
Color	Yellow
Location	Slightly up from navel
Principle	Formation of being
Purpose	This is where the personality is formed. Feeling and being are integrated here.
Element	Fire
Gems	Amber, Tiger's eye, Citrine, Yellow Topaz, Agate
Oils	Chamomile Lemon, Thyme
Sense	Sight
Effect	Eases aggression, pacifies
Aura	Mental Body
Body parts	Abdomen, lower back, stomach, spleen, liver, digestive system, gall bladder, autonomic nervous system, pancreas
Massage direction female	Counter-clockwise
Massage direction male	Clockwise
Mantra	Ram
Tone	E
Zodiac and planets	Leo, Sagittarius, Virgo, Sun, Jupiter, Mars, Mercury

Chakra	4 - ANAHATA (Heart)
Symbol	12 petaled Lotus
Color	Green
Location	Center of chest
Principle	Loving beyond the self
Purpose	The ability to love without fear and self-consciousness
Element	Air
Gems	Emerald, Green Jade, Rose Quartz
Oils	Geranium, Bergamot, Rose, Clary Sage
Sense	Touch
Effect	Brings peace and understanding
Aura	Astral Body
Body parts	Heart, upper back, rib cage, chest, skin, circulatory system, lower lungs, abdominal cavity, thymus gland
Massage direction female	Clockwise
Massage direction male	Counter-clockwise
Mantra	Yam
Tone	F
Zodiac and planets	Leo, Libra, Sun, Venus, Saturn

Chakra	5 - VISHUDDHA (Throat)
Symbol	16 petaled Lotus
Color	Light blue
Location	Between inner collarbone
Principle	Expression of being
Purpose	Deals with all related to sound, both physical and metaphysical
Element	Ether
Gems	Aquamarine, Turquoise, Chalcedony
Oils	Lavender, Sandalwood, Neroli, Sage
Sense	Sound
Effect	Brings harmony to speech and voice
Aura	Divine Will
Body parts	Lungs, vocal cords, bronchioles, throat, jaw, neck, thyroid, voice, nape of neck, thyroid gland
Massage direction female	Counter-clockwise
Massage direction male	Clockwise
Mantra	Ham
Tone	G
Zodiac and planets	Gemini, Taurus, Aquarius, Mars, Venus, Uranus

Chakra	6 - AJNA (Third Eye)
Symbol	96 petaled Lotus
Color	Indigo
Location	Between the eyes
Principle	Knowing of being
Purpose	This chakra enables the recognition of being
Element	All elements
Gems	Lapis Lazuli, Sodalite, Opal, Indigo Sapphire
Oils	Basil, Jasmine, Rosemary Patchouli
Sense	All plus 6th sense
Effect	Understanding, harmony
Aura	Celestial body
Body parts	Face, nose, eyes, sinus, cerebellum, pituitary gland
Massage direction female	Clockwise
Massage direction male	Counter-clockwise
Mantra	Kshama
Tone	A
Zodiac and planets	Sagittarius, Aquarius, Pisces, Mercury, Venus, Uranus

Chakra	7 - SAHASRARA (Crown)
Symbol	1000 petaled Lotus
Color	Violet, white
Location	Top and center of head
Principle	Pure being
Purpose	Here the human being connects with the Universe
Element	All elements
Gems	Amethyst, Crystal, Topaz, Alexandrite, Sapphire
Oils	Frankincense, Olibanum, Oakmoss, Lotus
Sense	Beyond senses
Effect	Cosmic aspect – no self-limitations
Aura	Ketheric Template
Body parts	Brain, cerebellum, skull, pineal gland
Massage direction female	Counter-clockwise
Massage direction male	Clockwise
Mantra	Om
Tone	Hum
Zodiac and planets	Capricorn, Pisces, Saturn, Neptune

Case Study 1

Fibromyalgia
Letting Go of the Pain Once and for All
by Carissa Lovgren

There is no relief in sight. I am always going to feel like this. Oh great! Another medication that will do nothing but leave me with unwanted side effects! This was my line of thinking, my reality.

In the spring and summer of 2006, I had been falling asleep in the middle of the day, I struggled to stand long enough to cook my family a dinner, and the pain ... the pain continued to get worse and worse. After every standard test was done and came back negative, the conclusion for Fibromyalgia. I was given a prescription for Lyrica and sent home.

Weeks went by and no relief. After several visits to the doctor over the following months I ended up on narcotic pain medication. First, we started out with Tylenol/codeine which gave me headaches, then we tried Vicodin, Darvocet and eventually landed on 5mg oxycodone (Percocet). There I stayed for several years. After two years, Lyrica made me sick as if I had a bad case of the flu, and was discontinued. So other than a daily multiple vitamin, oxycodone was my only treatment against the terrible pain and fatigue.

I was taking six pills per day and dealing with the side effects, like drowsiness, lightheadedness, constipation, weight gain, among others. In nearly ten years, I had gone from around 140 pounds ballooning up to 228 pounds at my heaviest and had taken up to practically living on the couch. I applied for and was granted Social Security Disability, so the opportunity to move from the bed to the couch and back to bed became my norm. Between the "Fibro" and the oxycodone, I had little to no energy. I was in pain every day, cried often and watched my kids pull away, and my husband leave me. I hit an all-time low.

That's when my father, Jon Lovgren, stepped in and introduced me to ho'oponopono. He outlined it as a lifestyle choice to heal all that afflicted me, through forgiveness. It's a simple phrase: "I love you, I'm sorry, Please forgive me, Thank you," and has powerful, life-altering effects. My father urged me to say it every time I thought about it or had an "uh-oh" or "what if" moment. Even if I didn't understand it at first – I just had to say it.

By now, I had anxiety so bad that it developed into Agoraphobia. My father and I started with two sessions a week, and at times, even had daily phone calls to address my severe anxiety before healing anything else, knowing that ho'oponopono was going to heal me in ways that I may not have been fully aware of in the meantime.

At first, I didn't think that it would work. How could forgiving myself for something that I did twenty years ago, heal my Agoraphobia if that only started a few years ago? Would saying a phrase repeatedly get me off the couch? I have always trusted my father, but I had my doubts.

Still, I did as encouraged and said the phrase all day, every day and cut the aka cords. Slowly changes began happening. I was able to pick up my daughter from school. I was able to go to the store and buy milk. Then, I was able to walk into a Wal-Mart – alone. Through the practice of ho'oponopono, I regained my confidence and a better understanding of where my anxiety came from. After some time and astounding healing, I decided that it was time to start work on my Fibro. With newly regained freedom, I felt the desire to get out more and more and eventually, possibly find a job.

We started with identifying when my Fibro started and were able to go back to a 2001 car accident … five years before my diagnosis. My father guided me in clearing that. As soon as I had, I broke down into sobs, but I went to bed that night feeling hopeful and lighter.

Over the next year or so, I worked at healing my body and my spirit. After several months I was down to four pain pills from six and I was more active. Having healed my Agoraphobia left me with wanting to always be somewhere, as we do not live right in town, you have to drive ten to fifteen minutes to find civilization. Although we had school bus service, I often picked up my daughter from school and would go out and run errands anywhere from half an hour to two hours, depending on our needs and if I wanted to stop by my library. I had even begun to return home from those trips and cook a full meal.

Working with ho'oponopono continued, as did the healing. In complete honesty, it probably would have taken less time if I had been able to remember to say it more often, but I am human. The point was, I was making progress and feeling really good. Integrating such a practice in my daily life became easy when results were staring me in the face.

Over a year had passed since I started using ho'oponopono and one day I was out running errands and becoming increasingly frustrated at how difficult it was to get in and out of the vehicle and my struggle to lift items like dog food or cat litter. I decided right there that I was going to join a gym and lose the weight.

After some searching, I applied for financial assistance at my community YMCA, which was granted, and I now pay an affordable rate for many amenities, including a pool, and a hot tub for those achy days. My daughter is covered under my membership too!

I started out walking on the treadmill for half an hour and then did some exercises on the yoga ball. I left there feeling great and went back the next day and even the day after that. Every time that I'd feel sore, I would say ho'oponopono, cut the cords and press on. Going to the gym became easier as the days passed.

A week went by, then two. I was still taking my oxycodone but noticed that I missed a dose once or twice, resulting in my only taking three per day. I decided to stick with that and see where it got me. After three weeks of going to the gym four to five times per week and having changed my eating habits completely, I felt stronger, I had lost five pounds, and consistently only took three oxycodone a day and at times would even forget to do that! I was feeling incredible.

Yes, I had days where I was fatigued and sore, but it was a different kind of sore, or different kind of tired. It didn't feel like the life-crushing pain that I had felt for so many years. On those days I would pause to say ho'oponopono, cut the aka cords and fill my heart and head with gratitude for how things were coming along. This time, I was tired from pushing myself a little more each time I went to the gym, from getting home and taking the dog for a walk, from successfully lifting a bag of dog food and carrying it all the way into the house. These victories began to add up and it kept me motivated and excited to continue my venture.

Today, four months later, I have a set workout schedule four times a week, I work out at home on the days that I don't go to the gym, and I have lost thirty pounds! I feel incredible, I have energy that I did not know that I was capable of and I say ho'oponopono every day all day. In a recent conversation with my father he caught me saying, "… when I used to have Fibromyalgia." I hadn't even realized that I said it! When he, ever the careful, attentive listener, repeated it back to me, I shrugged and said, "Yep, sounds about right!"

Ho'oponopono, when used, can be very powerful and absolutely life-changing. I healed years and years of pain both physical and spiritual, recovered relationships, recovered my freedom and have taken strides toward living a happy, healthy, anxiety- and pain-free life. I am so grateful for what ho'oponopono is doing in my life and for curing the "incurable."

Case Study 2

Fibromyalgia
Transcript of Talk Story Example

This is the transcript from a phone conversation with my daughter on or about February 9, 2017. This is a good example of how a talk story session may go. We start out talking about what is going on today and then through conversation and ho'oponopono we can trace the pain memories back to their origin.

Once we find the origin and heal that, the pain typically subsides very quickly, although it can take longer, which usually indicates there is still some healing to do around the incident or incidents.

Carissa is a good example of that – as I said, this conversation was in February 2017 and it was not until about a year later that I heard Carissa refer to Fibromyalgia in the past tense. YaY!!!

She continued this kind of work on her own with periodic talk story sessions. It has been about a year since she no longer had any of the symptoms and she is still doing well. Amazing, actually. She has lost I think about 60 pounds, goes the gym or exercises every day. Continues to practice ho'oponopono on a regular basis and has changed her diet.

In the end it seems that healing Fibromyalgia is a complete lifestyle change. And this is where perhaps ho'oponopono shines the brightest – lifestyle changes. The more we practice ho'oponopono, the more we learn to love ourselves and the more we love ourselves, the more we want to just naturally take better care of ourselves.

As I remember, this conversation was approximately an hour and a half long. I typically schedule talk story sessions for two hours.

Jon: What did we want to talk about today?

Carissa: Let's talk about pain and how to get past it.

Jon: When you're in pain, is there a specific point or place in your body where it shows up? Or is it all over?

Carissa: It's quite widespread. If I've been sitting or lying down for too long, my legs hurt worse than anything else. My hips are real bad.

Jon: Are you exercising much?

Carissa: Not much, but I am doing yoga and I work on the yoga ball.

Jon: The idea of going to the mall and walking would be good for your hips and your legs. Right?

Carissa: Yes.

Jon: The longer the better, but, starting out, at least 20 minutes, a half-hour maybe. Walk up the hill and back down or walk down the hill and back up.

Carissa: It's not real safe this time of year with people flying down the road, but I can go into town and find a place. I can walk Market Street.

Jon: Yeah, but don't stroll, you have to walk. Not walking and stopping and shopping. Walk down to the Denison Avenue sidewalk. Start at one end and go all the way up and then walk back down Market Street maybe a little slower. And just start making that circle, right? Do you go into town every day?

Carissa: No.

Jon: You could though, right?

Carissa: Yeah, about 95% of the time I could.

Jon: I would strongly suggest that you walk as much as you can. Start with that circuit, even if you only do half. Start there and work your way up because you don't want to go too far and end up being sore and adding to the pain.

Carissa: Right.

Jon: And you're drinking lots of water?

Carissa: Oh, tons. All day, every day.

Jon: That would help your hips.

Carissa: Yeah. Well, we have a Wii and there's a Fit Plus on it with a balance board, and so I do marching and stepping and stuff that works my hips too, so I do that on days that I'm home. That helps.

Jon: The outside walking is better than walking in place.

Carissa: In the summer there's Hornby State Park right up the road. I can go on the trails. They're pretty level.

Jon: Well, yeah, by this time next year. You need to build up your strength first, and your stamina, and that will be easiest on a level surface.

Carissa: Right.

Jon: You know, people have a tendency to say, I'm gonna work out, and then they go work out and overdo it trying to get buff in a couple days instead of a couple months, and they end up getting sore and they quit doing it. So you just gotta ease into it. It's one of those things that you keep doing 'till you like doing it. I used to walk for miles. Mostly 'cause I didn't have a car. (laughs) That always helps. But nonetheless, I always enjoyed walking 'cause it's a good meditation space. And, you know, stupid stuff will come up, of course, so you'll want to be more cognizant of ho'oponopono. Right? So as soon as any stupid stuff comes up, you just start ho'oponopono until it's gone.

Carissa: Yes.

Jon: But typically, walking is a relaxing, meditative thing, but it also seems to get us thinking, too. A lot of people walk to think things out. So, when you're walking, just look around. Notice the buildings, the houses, the trees, and it won't take long, and you'll start to notice differences, and at some point, if you do it long enough, you'll start to see daily differences, if you look close enough. Just go learn the town you live in, you know.

Carissa: Right.

Jon: You haven't seen it from a different perspective, so when we walk, we have a tendency to notice more what's around us and listen to the sounds. How many sounds can you hear at any given time, like you hear traffic, a loud muffler, birds, people talking. Focus in on how many sounds you are hearing as you walk. That will start to activate and open up your pineal gland and your third eye a little bit too. And so when that starts happening, and you start to be able to notice that stuff when you're driving by as well, you start to be able to come into the moment easier.

Carissa: Yes.

Jon: Is it painful to walk or not so much?

Carissa: Yeah. It's very painful.

Jon: Oh, well then you really gotta start slow.

Carissa: I usually end up limping.

Jon: Well, don't limp very far. In fact, if you start limping, then just stop and take a break.

Carissa: It's that left hip that does it to me. I get cortisone injections in my hip. I stopped getting injections, but I used to because it hurt so bad.

Jon: Do you know the cause?

Carissa: Well, the fibromyalgia. He says that I spend too much time on that hip, that I sleep on that hip. He says people end up sleeping on that hip too long, and they don't turn over in the night and it hurts them throughout the day. He says the only thing he can think of is that it's fibromyalgia.

Jon: Did they do X-rays or MRIs or anything?

Carissa: No. He asked me if there was an injury or if I'd fallen or anything like that and I said no. It just gradually came on and started hurting, and walking makes it worse, and sitting, leaning on it makes it worse.

Jon: Well, I would suggest if you sleep on the left hip that you start sleeping on the right hip.

Carissa: I do, but I turn over at night and don't know it until I wake up in pain and then I turn back over to my right. But I've been doing my best to train myself to stay off that hip when I sleep, but I move around a lot.

Jon: How's your hip right now? Does it hurt?

Carissa: No. I'm not on it.

Jon: Do you have any pain anywhere?

Carissa: Yes, a dull ache all over. My back. My neck.

Jon: Can you find a position that will fire up that hip pain?

Carissa: Yeah, I can lay on it.

Jon: Just lean on it.

Carissa: All I gotta do is lay on it for five minutes.

Jon: Does it go away pretty quick when you get off of it?

Carissa: Sometimes it aches for a while. But, yeah, I'm on the hip now, and just waiting for it to get sore. If it hurts me, I'll just get off it, that's all.

Jon: Yeah, we won't stay very long, I just want to walk through a process that I go through when the pain comes up. And when did your fibro start? 2006?

Carissa: That's when it was diagnosed, but it started 2 years before that when I was pregnant.

Jon: Okay. So, take a nice deep breath. Just relax. Let's go back to the first time you remember feeling it. Where in your body did you feel it and what did it feel like?

Carissa: It mostly felt like muscle fatigue.

Jon: Any particular area of the body?

Carissa: I slept a lot when I was first pregnant, and that's when I noticed it in my arms when I would reach for something, and I think probably even in my legs. He lived in the second floor apartment and one day I just had to stop going up the stairs and take a rest, and I didn't used to have to do that.

Jon: And what was he like through the pregnancy?

Carissa: He was not sympathetic. He would yell at me and tell me to get off my ass and go get a job but yet he would sit at home and play on the computer all day and would not go get a job.

Jon: Is any of this starting to click for you? So, let's ponder this. So, you're pregnant and the daddy's zero support through the whole pregnancy and mean on top of that basically, yeah?

Carissa: Yes.

Jon: Did you ever have any thoughts of what am I doing here, I can't do this anymore, I need to get out of this?

Carissa: Oh, yeah. Constantly. I remember one time specifically.

Jon: Can you describe that time?

Carissa: I was on the phone with my mother and I was begging her to wire me some money for gas so that I could drive my vehicle from Syracuse back to Buffalo so that I could look into the possibility of getting an abortion because I was so desperate for all the fighting to stop, and I was so desperate to feel better emotionally and physically that I was thinking that that's got to be the only answer and could she please help me because I'm stuck in Syracuse and I don't want to be in this situation anymore.

Jon: Okay. And so, just step back a little bit prior to that. How did it happen that you got pregnant? I mean, you didn't plan it.

Carissa: No, it wasn't planned. We met and started hanging out, and it just progressed. I was on birth control.

Jon: Oh, wow, that worked really well. Ugh!

Carissa: We worked for the same company, he worked out of Syracuse and I worked in Buffalo, and we started hanging out, and the company paid for him to have a hotel room twice a week for his deliveries and stuff and I would go visit him in the hotel and we'd watch movies and eat Chinese take-out and whatever and one night we kissed and then things progressed from there.

Jon: When you found out you were pregnant, what was your reaction?

Carissa: I wasn't surprised. I already knew, 'cause I knew my body and I knew what was going on in my body. So, it was just like oh, okay, yeah.

Jon: Ultimately, we have to step into responsibility for ourselves and how we created that for ourselves, yeah?

Carissa: Yeah.

Jon: Can you find a space in there that you can own the responsibility for creating that situation? You know what I mean, right?

Carissa: I can go back further than that, because had I not done certain things, then I wouldn't have ended up in Syracuse in the first place. It ended up being a bad situation, and then he gave me an out by saying why don't you just move to Syracuse with me, and that's what we did.

Jon: Okay, so that's probably when the timing was. So you feel like moving to Syracuse at that point was a bad decision?

Carissa: Yes, I do.

Jon: Okay. Go back to that, feel into that decision phase. You made a decision, right, because you were reacting, not responding. And, you know, love yourself. Ho'oponopono. I love you. I'm sorry that I created that situation. I didn't understand at the time, that's what was going to happen, I'm so sorry I made that decision, please forgive me for doing that. Thank you. Now I have more understanding.

Jon: How does that feel right now? Any relief?

Carissa: I feel surrounded by yellow.

Jon: Is that comforting?

Carissa: Yes.

Jon: So, that would be an indication to me that there's something going on there. You were living from your solar plexus, your lower chakras, rather than from your heart. How does that feel? That feeling of yellow. Is it comforting, or not so much?

Carissa: Mildly, yeah. It feels familiar.

Jon: Yeah, I imagine. I expect that more as we go along, we're gonna find out a lot more places where there's a similar situation, similar feelings are gonna come up, yeah. But this is a big one, in regard to your fibro.

Jon: So, you put yourself in that position and now you've accepted responsibility for doing so, and there's no part of it that's just your fault, right? Because one of our theses is that we're each 100 percent responsible for everything in our lives. So, when we fully embrace and embody that, there is no more blame.

Carissa: Right.

Jon: So, you cannot blame just you anymore for anything, right? Does that make sense?

Carissa: Yes.

Jon: Okay. So, that was your responsibility for initiating that and getting in that situation and forgiving yourself, and you love yourself for it. And that's gonna release a whole bunch of stuff for you. And so, we go into what you feel now and feeling surrounded by yellow. Can you feel into that more? Go back and be real vulnerable again about making that decision to move through it and see if you can get there from your heart, feel into it. Just feel it.

Carissa: I don't know, I feel like something keeps stopping it.

Jon: Yeah. Is there any sadness or anger? When you think about that decision, what kind of feeling comes up initially?

Carissa: Fear.

Jon: And what's the fear?

Carissa: Fear of the unknown. Leaving what I know in Buffalo to go to a whole new city.

Jon: So, don't hold onto that fear, because it was unnecessary. Right? It was unnecessary. Moving to a new city and everything was fine at the time. Or better.

Jon: Take a nice, deep breath. And now, how do you feel? Different than a few minutes ago?

Carissa: Warm.

Jon: Is that comfortable?

Carissa: Yeah. Still feeling it.

Jon: Wow. Good job.

Jon:	And now, remember when we talked about how you felt yellow?
Carissa:	Yeah.
Jon:	Is the yellow still there, or has that changed?
Carissa:	This sounds funny, but it's kind of like Swiss cheese now. As in warm and kind of like more powerful, it's more strong.
Jon:	Yeah. Go back to that place of fear again, yeah?
Carissa:	Okay.
Jon:	And what was one thing you were afraid of?
Carissa:	Not having any money 'cause I left my job.
Jon:	So the fear of not having any money. Go back into there. Feel into that, remember what that felt like.
Carissa:	Okay.
Jon:	And how do you feel now?
Carissa:	Better.
Jon:	How's the yellow?
Carissa:	Barely there.
Jon:	What was another fear you had at that time?
Carissa:	Being able to take care of Hannah.

Jon: Go back into there, feel into that, how that felt. And again, now in this moment.

Carissa: Feeling a lot of blue. The yellow's gone, but I'm feeling a lot of blue now.

Jon: All right, cool. Blue's your throat chakra, right? So, first thing, you took care of Hannah in spite of the move.

Carissa: Right.

Jon: So does this kind of make sense now? How ho'oponopono works? How we change the yellow, the solar plexus, ego, the energy around you, in front of you? And now, come to the throat? Yeah?

Carissa: Yes.

Jon: And how it feels better?

Carissa: Yeah, I feel more comfortable.

Jon: So now, imagine yourself having a conversation with Hannah today. In this year. Presently. And imagine that you explain to her. How old was she at that point?

Carissa: Back then? Like three.

Jon: Three or four, so she probably doesn't remember too much about it. Maybe she does. So, check in and see what it would feel like if you had a little conversation with her right now in your mind, yeah? And, you know, just tell her how much you love her and how happy you are that she stuck by your side all this time and the gratitude that you have that you were able to take care of her appropriately.

Carissa: Okay.

Jon: They're not my words, but they reside in you. How's that feeling, still got the blue?

Carissa: Not really there.

Jon: Any other changes?

Carissa: The top of my head is tingling. I don't know if that's relevant, but it started not too long ago.

Jon: So, breathe that in, breathe it into your heart, yeah? Breathe it in again. Bring it down to your heart. And bring it in and fill your body with it.

Jon: And exhale it from your heart. And one more. Breathe it in and fill your body, and exhale through the heart.

Carissa: I'm lightheaded. I'm laying down too. It's weird.

Jon: How's the tingling?

Carissa: I can still feel a little bit of it.

Jon: Feel pink at all?

Carissa: No, it's white.

Jon: So, are you recognizing the changes that are going on here? A little bit?

Carissa: Yeah, a little bit.

Jon: I just wanna point out that this is where ho'oponopono starts coming into the language of it all, yeah? Cause you're now communicating with your unconscious mind, and it's showing you these little signs that its paying attention, like giving you the yellow color surrounding you. Your third chakra. And then you did more work with ho'oponopono and that changed, you know? You punched holes in the yellow by eliminating another fear, and got rid of it completely by eliminating the third fear, yeah?

Jon: And then it went to blue, which is your throat chakra, which is an indicator that something's stuck in your throat chakra. You need to speak your truth. Or, you have something that needs to be said.

Jon: And so by having that conversation with Hannah, you were able to say some of the things that you needed to say to her that maybe she's never heard. I mean, I don't know the conversation, nor do I need to. But when you have that conversation then that blue dissipated as well, right?

Carissa: Yes.

Jon: So, the unconscious is telling us that those fears were in your solar plexus and you poked holes in that and worked through that, and then it moves up to your throat, letting us know that you just transformed from fear into needing to say something. Right?

Jon: And when you talked it out you released that fear. And then the tingling in the head and the crown chakra is potentially your spirit or source of your higher self recognizing that you're doing this work, yeah?

Jon: And pink is the color of love, often. Like, rose quartz. And so, by focusing on breathing in the love of the creator through your crown chakra and filling your body with it, and then sending it out your heart, you're clearing out all of that shit that's in you, you know?

Carissa: Right.

Jon: Those old limiting beliefs that no longer serve, yeah? And so when you did that in those four breaths, the color of the crown chakra is white. So, when it changed from pink to white, the source is letting you know that, you know what, that's like a thank you for paying attention to what I was giving you. The awareness. Does that make sense?

Carissa: Yeah. Yeah, it does.

Jon: And so, you've been laying on your hip for, I don't know how long it's been, five, ten minutes. And I didn't hear any indication of it starting to hurt. Is it hurting now?

Carissa: No, it's fine.

Jon: That doesn't surprise me. Does it surprise you?

Carissa: A little.

Jon: So, what's going on there is that when your hip starts hurting, just in general, that becomes your focus, yeah?

Carissa: Right.

Jon: And my guess is, from my experience in pain, that when that pain starts, it's like, "Oh here we go again. Just stop. Please stop. God, please stop." You know? All we want it to do is stop, yeah? And so what's happening there is, here we come into one of my biggest lessons lately. What we resist persists. So the more that we resist that pain, the stronger it's gonna get. And, when it gets stronger there, and you're still resisting it, it starts moving around your body and through the body.

Jon: And then it goes up your back, and you know, you have fibromyalgia basically.

Jon: So, yeah. Pay attention to these things. Maybe you make a little sign, put it on the wall somewhere, "What we resist persists," until you get that. And when you get that, as soon as you start to feel pain, you recognize, "Oh, what we resist persists. So, rather than resisting it, let me go in and see what it is trying to tell me."

Carissa: Yeah. Yeah.

Jon: So, today it was telling us that, "Well, I did some stupid shit a number of years ago that I forgot about basically, 'cause life goes on." And as we're doing ho'oponopono in the moment through the pain, we can pretty quickly get back to the originating time of it and how it came to be. Does that make sense?

Carissa: Yep.

Jon: We stop resisting it and we start loving the pain because it's really a communicator. It's just a messenger. It's telling us that we need to pay attention to something here. And if you're not gonna pay attention to it, and if you're gonna fight me on it, I'm gonna make it worse. Rather than continuing to resist it, or take medication to stop it, cause all that really does is put you to sleep, and mask it, it gets you distracted and it's not helping any, ultimately.

Carissa: Is fatigue the same as pain, as far as telling you something?

Jon: It comes down to why are you fatigued. And is it a chronic thing, or is it just acute? If it's acute because you ran your ass crazy all day long and not much sleep? Or is it fatigue?

Carissa: Yeah, I get it. I mean like, sleep all night, wake up, and two hours later you're ready for a nap 'cause you're so fricking tired and you don't know why.

Jon: Well, that's ultimately the same thing. When you lay around, lay around, lay around, that's all you wanna do. Lay around, lay around. That's how depression often starts. And how that escalates, you know? So that's why it's important to get out and go for a walk, especially if you can do it outside.

Carissa: I like being outside.

Jon: And, when you're going for the walk, practice being mindful, like we talked about. Notice the thing that's going on, and when you feel the breeze, if there's a breeze, feeling into the breeze. And, if you meditate and feel into the breeze, at some point you may be able to feel it blowing through you instead of around you.

Carissa: That's pretty cool.

Jon: It is cool. When you start to feel that way, that feels really good, so that's a good example of being in the flow. You're so in the flow that the breeze can blow through you. You're right in it, yeah?

Carissa: I've had that happen to me before, actually. I know what you're talking about. It is pretty cool. It happened with the mist coming off a waterfall.

Jon: And then, you can feel the water flowing through you, like in the shower even?

Carissa: Yeah. I have to be around water. That's my thing. I think that's why I drink so much of it.

Jon: Yeah, it could be. Swimming from the inside out. So, you sound like you're feeling better.

Carissa: Yeah, I'm not as tired. I feel lighter, a little bit. I don't know if that makes sense, but I just got up to walk around a little bit and I don't feel so heavy on my feet.

Jon: Yup. And now, the other thing is that you're gonna have a tendency to do is you're gonna check in with the hip. Like, when I did this for my back and the back pain went away right away. It might have even been weeks. Every once in a while, it started out probably every day and then it kept going, and I kept thinking, "Well darn it, my back used to hurt when I did this. But now it's not hurting anymore. Oh, okay, cool." But we don't wanna sink into it too much, we can bring that back because it's so familiar.

Jon: But, by the same token, we can understand that we just created it in this moment by doing that. So, when we start to think about the hip, then we just automatically go into ho'oponopono and get rid of the thoughts so we're no longer thinking about that, what it used to be.

Carissa: Yes.

Jon: And I wouldn't be a bit surprised if your hip is a lot better if not completely better in the next few days, and maybe forever.

Carissa: That'd be great.

Jon: What came to me, with my back, was at one point after, I was like, "Holy shit, I can't remember the last time I even thought about my back hurting."

Carissa: Right. Yeah. Right.

Jon: So, just because we do ho'oponopono doesn't mean that whole thing changes. The emotional grief that caused the pain is gone, so there's no reason for the pain anymore, right? And so we can always recreate that reasoning any time we want to. And I do it all the time. I was on these retreats for a couple weeks and then I went to a music festival last weekend for three days. And, you know, almost three days of sitting on the ground on pillows or squatting. Sitting on the ground makes my back sore, plain and simple.

Carissa: Right.

Jon: But the pain feels familiar like it used to. Like it used to send me to the doctor. But now that I know what it is, it's just like, "Well, I don't exercise enough. I don't have a very strong back at this point in time. I'm signing up for yoga soon. I'm gonna start to rebuild my core strength. But the point is that I knew why that pain was there. It wasn't from old injuries and old memories and old stupid stuff, right? It was because I was not treating my body as good as I could. And so it would ache a little bit and I might think about laying down or going for a walk or doing something other than just sitting on the ground, yeah?

Jon: And so I would get up and go for a walk or find a blanket somewhere, just lay in the grass for a little while listening to music, yeah? And of course as soon as I took the pressure off of it, it went away. There's no more chronic pain. We're pretty much always gonna have moments of pain when we do stupid stuff or we're not paying attention. But there's no more chronic pain. So this brings awareness to what you might expect in the next few days or weeks. And if the hip pain does come back like you were describing it earlier, then again, what we resist, persists. As soon as you hear that in your mind, you immediately go into ho'oponopono and you go back to that scenario that we just talked about. And there's a lot more there than just the three things we worked through today.

Carissa: Yeah.

Jon: Because how long were you with him? The whole pregnancy?

Carissa: No. Six months. But we were involved for two months prior to that.

Jon: Right. So just to say that there's a lot of memories attached to that. We only got a couple of them today. So you can't expect to go get a couple and it's gonna completely heal it. Unless you can get back to the very root cause of it, then it helps. But when my back hurts from sitting, working too long, whatever, oftentimes I'll just ho'oponopono and check in with myself and go see if there are other memories attached to that. Or if it's just in today's bad posture or whatever. Does that make sense?

Carissa: Yes.

Jon: So that's pretty cool, huh?

Carissa: Yeah. I'm thinking about what we're talking about while we're talking about it. So I'm processing right now.

Jon: How's your hip?

Carissa: It's fine. I got up and walked around for a little bit because the rest of me was getting sore, but I sat back down and I'm all right.

Jon: So it's different than it was an hour ago or two hours ago or yesterday.

Carissa: Yes, earlier today.

Jon: So that's really the beginning. That's what we're looking for. The change, yeah? And if you remember, we talked about neuroplasticity, right? How when we do this, it changes the molecules in our brain.

Jon: So you did that long enough today. Based on Abraham's teachings, if you could hold a thought for 17 seconds, it creates that cell in the brain basically. And if you can hold it for, I think it's some ridiculous 57 seconds, but basically for 60 seconds, then it becomes implanted in the brain. And then if you continue to hold that thought, it continues to grow and get stronger. And then it starts replacing those low vibrations, negative thought patterns that are stuck in there.

Jon: And so you continue to do that whenever you feel the hip pain, immediately ho'oponopono it. And what you're doing at the physiological, physical level is changing your brain structure, teaching it that you love your hip, you're sorry you mistreated it. Please forgive me for doing that. Oftentimes I just didn't know better at the time, but now I understand. Thank you for that understanding.

Jon: And then pretty soon you'll realize that you're no longer doing ho'oponopono around your hip because your hip just doesn't bother you anymore.

Carissa: Right.

Jon: The same process applies throughout the body.

Carissa: Yeah. That's what I'm thinking. Like my neck or something like that.

Jon: Right. And you know, I had a bumpy pillow at the retreat center for two or three weeks. So oftentimes I'd wake up with a stiff neck. And those old thoughts would come in, like I gotta take a pill. Where did that come from? But I don't have those thoughts so much anymore. But every once in a while, they come up. And it was a good indicator to me that I better ho'oponopono this. And so I do. I go into the neck. And most of the time, there's no emotional aspect to it really. It's just that I got a bad pillow and I slept funny and everybody wakes up with a stiff neck once in a while.

Jon: I suppose I could go into why do I sleep funny? Why do I create a stiff neck unconsciously, yeah? And there's probably something to that, right? Because when we pay attention to that, then I'm more apt to make sure I have a better pillow. Or a bit more apt to make sure I'm lying in a better position so that doesn't happen. But when we get so tired all we want to do is get horizontal. Just as soon as I hit the pillow, I'm asleep.

Carissa: Yeah. I'm doing what I can to train myself to move in certain ways and not sleep in certain positions throughout the night. Because I wake up so many times throughout the night. This hurts, that hurts. You know, I slept on this too long or whatever. And I'm doing what I can to try to get that into my subconscious so that I don't wake up every time it happens. And that if I'm on one side too long, that I'll just turn over or I'll go on my back or whatever.

Carissa: And so that's been my struggle the past couple of weeks, is sleep training myself in a way.

Jon: Are you seeing any differences since you've had this?

Carissa: Well I still wake up. But I know that if I've been on one side too long, it takes me a long time to move over to another position. And I used to get really, really frustrated. And I'd get pissed and I'd throw the covers and I'd thrash about and kind of flop into the next position. But now, I just say okay, so this is happening. And I take a deep breath. And I'm able to move a lot more fluidly into an alternative position. So I'm not as frustrated or upset about it. I also am not waking up as much.

Jon: So it's working then.

Carissa: I think it is working. Yeah. But I wake up in the morning and I'm still so sore. And it takes me forever to get out of bed. And then I stand up and I have to stand for a couple of minutes before I take a step. You know, some mornings are better than others. Some mornings I can lay in bed and stretch. So I think it's working.

Jon: Sounds like it. If you like where you're at or getting what you're getting, then keep doing what you're doing. Your hip is changing for the better. And again, it comes back to being mindful of it. And so from now on actually, when you lie down to go to bed, when you go to sleep, just ho'oponopono. If you have the wherewithal in the middle of the night, when you wake up in pain, immediately start ho'oponopono again as you roll over or change positions, and then just repeat ho'oponopono until you fall back asleep. So you start building a habit of saying ho'oponopono every time you feel pain.

Carissa: Yeah.

Jon: And then when you have time to process a little more, then you can go through and do what we did today. You go in, you remember the pain that you had last night, whichever one. And you go into it. And do your best to remember the first time you felt it.

Carissa: What if the first time you remember is not the actual first time?

Jon: That's okay because that'll come back later. I've learned that so many times, I thought something was related to something 10 years before that or five years before that.

Carissa: Oh, okay, so it'll come back.

Jon: So that's the beauty of it. Ho'oponopono is a never-ending process and you're never gonna completely clear everything. You'll heal everything but you won't clear or clean all those memories. Because how many memories do we have from the beginning of time?

Carissa: And that goes beyond this particular life as well.

Jon: Well yeah. That's my point. Since the beginning of time, I have no idea how many lives we had. Even if all of them are on this planet. They might all have been somewhere else too. We don't know. Anyway, we could go on a whole different direction in that.

Carissa: Oh yeah, I know.

Jon: Ah, I wouldn't be surprised that as you're clearing this pain, at some point as you keep going back with it, some of it's gonna point to your mother and some of it's gonna point to me. Situations and interactions with us in the past.

Carissa: I've encountered that already.

Jon: So you're carrying some of our pain with you as I'm carrying some of my parents' and grandparents' pain with me.

Jon: So to say we're gonna go back to the origin of it 100 percent is not very likely. But we can get back to the origin of it in our current lives, in our current physical form, yeah?

Carissa: Yeah.

Jon: And I worked with one person one time and she went back and cleared stuff while she was still in the womb. It was pretty crazy.

Carissa: That's Hannah right there. She'll be able to do something like that. Because she remembers stuff from when she was a year old and it drives me wild. It's amazing.

Jon: Yeah. Well she's fifteen so it's easier for her to remember a year old, than it is for either of us.

Jon: Does this all make sense, sweetie?

Carissa: Yeah. And it's very helpful. It's definitely started to lay the foundation under which I'm going to completely abolish my fibromyalgia and no longer have it.

Jon: There you go. Yeah, baby. That's what I'm talking about.

Carissa: That's what tonight's conversation did.

Jon: Awesome. Whew. That was my hope. So this is gonna go away. The only work it takes is what we did today. You're just gonna have to do that consistently.

Carissa: Yeah. I got time.

Jon: And it's kind of cool because now that you've got a good foundation as you say, it's gonna go away at an exponential rate, yeah? So the more of it you do, the faster it's gonna heal and the faster it's gonna dissipate and the better you're gonna feel. And then next month you'll come up on Friday waiting for meds and you won't give two shits. Like, I don't care. I got meds left over because I'm not taking them anymore.

Carissa: Right.

Jon: Awesome. Thank you, sweetie.

Carissa: For what?

Jon: Oh it takes a lot of courage to go into this kind of stuff, yeah?

Carissa: Yeah.

Jon: A lot of people, for whatever reason, can't go into the within, is what it boils down to.

Carissa: Well I think I'm in a space where I'm ready to heal and I'm ready to not be in pain and I'm ready to not have fibromyalgia. You know, I think I'm there.

Jon: The willingness. And then the same question I asked your friend that one day is how willing and ready are you to let go of this pain? Can you answer it? How willing and ready are you to let go of fibromyalgia?

Carissa: Maybe 85, 90 percent ready.

Jon: Okay. That's good enough.

Carissa: I've been in constant pain for a month. I'm done.

Jon: I got a good lesson from your friend when I asked her that question, because she said, "Well as much as I want to say 100 percent, if that were true, I wouldn't have it in the first place." So maybe 80 percent was good enough and she canceled her surgery appointment, yeah?

Carissa: Yeah, yeah. It went away.

Jon: Because she was able to let go of it.

Carissa: Yep.

Jon: So you're at 85 or 90 percent. It makes perfect sense. So that's enough. You are on your way to freedom, sweetie.

Carissa: I like that word.

Jon: And on the fast track I might add.

Carissa: Is there such a thing as overdoing it? Can you do too much ho'oponopono and clear too much shit in one day?

Jon: Yeah. Boy howdy. I don't think so. I've tried and I can't get there.

Carissa: I mean I wouldn't want any mental exhaustion, but I could easily get off the phone with you right now. Hannah's occupied herself. I could do some more work once we get off the phone. And then after journaling tonight before bed, I can do some more work. You know?

Jon: You know what? That's like asking somebody if you can love somebody too much or is there too much love. Right? No you cannot overdo ho'oponopono. Because you know what the results of overdosing on ho'oponopono are?

Carissa: Couldn't be bad.

Jon: My life. No. My life is a good example of the results of overdosing on ho'oponopono, yeah? It's like I'm not only crazy and I laugh at everything anymore. I got into some stupid shit earlier this week, as a matter of fact. And in the moment, I was frustrated. And then after the situation was over and I was thinking about it, of course, analyzing it because that's what I do. Getting clear on why did I feel this and why did I take that personally and yada

yada yada. And then I understood the situation better, but I really don't get it completely. So let's do ho'oponopono. And I went in, worked with ho'oponopono and within 15 or 20 minutes, I'm laughing at the whole thing.

Jon: And understanding, and this is very important and crucial, that when we get in those kinds of situations, the biggest message I got was that was how the Universe was conspiring to make my desires and dreams come true for that moment. Does that make sense? Because you know what they say, that your desire, the Universe is always conspiring to give you what you ask for.

Carissa: Yeah. Yeah.

Jon: Right? And so what we don't understand in that statement is that when we're angry and mad and stomping our feet and throwing a fit, we're asking. Yeah, the calling and feeding? An example of calling and feeding is if you see a stray cat outside your house a few times and then all of a sudden you decide, "I think I want to make friends with that cat and have a pet."

Jon: So you set a food dish out and the cat comes around and starts eating. You're feeding the cat. So you're calling the cat to you. And then you go out a couple days later. Oy vey, there are six cats out there. I don't want six cats, I just want one. So you take the food away. You stop feeding it. And as a result, you stop calling in all the cats. And then you gradually set the dish out again and that same cat comes back. And you pay attention to it maybe every other day or something like that. And then, next thing you know, you have a pet.

Jon: Our feelings are cat food.

Jon: So that's what our feelings are, right? Whatever we're feeling, we're feeding out to the Universe, calling for more of that feeling. And the Universe responds in like and gives us exactly what we're feeding, what we're calling for. Does that make sense?

Carissa: Yes.

Jon: And so when we're in those angry lower vibration energies, we're feeding those to the Universe. We very quickly start to recognize that and immediately go into ho'oponopono. And stop those feelings and stop feeding that. And the Universe will go, "Okay. Never mind. I got other shit to do anyway." Because it's not as good as what we were asking for anymore.

Carissa: Yeah.

Jon: You can just get into a state and your immediate reaction is, "Oh shit!" Then the next reaction should be, "I love you, I'm sorry, please forgive me, and thank you. I love you, I'm sorry, please forgive me, thank you. I love you, I'm sorry, please forgive me, thank you."

Jon: Right? So that's my indicator. Because as much as I want ho'oponopono to be second nature, and it pretty much is for me, I still get in stupid stuff and my first response is, "Oh shit!"

Jon: But now I've learned as soon as I get that response, I immediately launch into ho'oponopono.

Carissa: That's my response when it comes to my anxiety and agoraphobia. "Oh, my concert's on Monday. Oh hell. What am I gonna do?" And I immediately went into that space.

Jon: So as soon as you go to that space, you go, "I love you, I'm sorry, please forgive me, thank you. I love you, I'm sorry, please forgive me, thank you." And you know, Monday's a long way away. So, if you do ho'oponopono on it, then you're not resisting it anymore. You're loving into it. And the Universe will conspire to make everything happen with grace and ease.

Jon: eh, aloha'aku, eh aloha mai.

Case Study 3

Thirty Years of Chronic Back Pain
Gone in an Instant

I had chronic low-back pain for over 30 years. I had multiple MRIs, facet joint injections, nerve blocks, everything but surgery. And I joined the pain management fiasco. Yes, for me it was a fiasco. I went through addiction and withdrawal numerous times.

The initial injury was from a construction accident and there were a couple of automobile accidents with MRIs showing bulging discs and pinched nerves.

About 4 years ago I was receiving an acupuncture treatment. The acupuncturist places the needles and leaves for about 20 minutes. During that time, I decided to practice ho'oponopono. I began repeating the mantra over and over:

> I love you
> I am sorry
> Please forgive me
> Thank you

And asking, "How did I create this for myself? And Why?"

As I continued to repeat the mantra, a memory surfaced of when I was 9 years old and my Dad was yelling at me and what I heard was, "You worthless piece of shit, you're never going to amount to anything!"

How do I accept responsibility for that?! I stepped back just prior to hearing that and accepted that whatever I had done, I hurt my Father a great deal. What parent wants to say something like that to their children?

In that moment I started crying as I felt into the pain my Father must have felt and I understood how deeply I had hurt him, and he was simply reacting. As we know from previous discussion, reaction is predominantly in the low-vibration, negative feelings.

I kept saying ho'oponopono. I love you. I am sorry I hurt my Dad do deeply and that I took on his anger and carried it with me throughout my life, I did not do it on purpose. Please forgive me for hurting him and for taking on that worthlessness. Thank you for showing me this. Thank you for loving me. Thank you for forgiving me.

The pain vanished in that instant and has not returned. Yes, my back still gets sore, but it is because I sit on the ground a lot. When my back hurts now, I understand it is simply my posture and when I change my posture, the pain goes away.

Another noteworthy memory connected to this. I used to say that all I remember hearing when growing up was "You are a worthless piece of shit; you will never amount to anything." I could not wait to get out of the house after graduating high school. In that same healing moment, I realized that I likely never heard those words again; however, when they were spoken the first time, I took them to heart and owned them 100%. After that, whenever Dad raised his voice or spoke in anger, those were the words I heard.

By remembering and cleaning the memory at 9 years old, it cleaned all the memories attached to it from that point forward, for example, hearing different words than were said. Now when people get angry with me, I hear what they say and not the words my Father spoke at 9 years old. Prior to this cleaning, when someone would get angry with me, the initial feeling for me was I am worthless. Now, having cleaned that memory, that is no longer the case, I can now hear the words as they are meant.

Case Study 4

Forty Years of Chronic Foot Pain
Gone Overnight

I met Tammy about 2 years ago at a retreat here on island. We participated in several retreats and came to be good friends.

One weekend I was scheduled to do a Talks Story Session on a Saturday afternoon. I asked Tammy if she would be willing to volunteer to walk through something so we could show the rest of the attendees the process. She agreed.

A little of Tammy's background: She was born with a deformed foot and had surgery at an early age. The foot did not heal correctly so she has had pain in her right foot most of her life, over 40 years. And... she spent most of her working life as a waitress in a casino in Las Vegas, Nevada. When I met her, she worked as a server at the busiest restaurant in Hilo, Hawai'i. So always on her feet.

We began talking story about "How did I create this for myself and why? Unfortunately, I do not have a transcript for this session. However, when all was said and done, the next day she came walking across the yard shaking her foot and laughing. She said, "I have to learn how to walk all over again, this is the first time in 40 years I have had no pain in my foot!"

Tammy was able to heal 4 generations through that process. She healed memories with herself, her daughter, her Mother, and her Grandmother. Another interesting side to this session happened about 2 hours after the session.

Tammy's Aunt lives in Germany. She called a couple of hours after our session and asked Tammy, "What is going on? You know German women are strong and never cry, but I just spent the last 2 hours crying and I do not know why!" Tammy explained what happened and her Aunt, even though she did not understand what happened, was relieved.

This is a testament to the aka cords. Tammy's love and healing traveled through all the aka cords attached to each person and as Tammy healed, the others received it as well.

It is now almost 2 years later, and Tammy is still going strong! She is no longer on island, and is sorely missed, but she is doing amazing things in Grass Valley, California. She is working as a server in a restaurant, gardening, and now she just established her first bee-hive. She is doing her part in changing the world by doing what she can to increase and maintain the bee population.

Thank you, Tammy! I love you so much!!!

About the Author

Jon Lovgren lives in Hawai'i and is an Ordained Minister, a Reiki Master/Teacher, Spiritual Life Coach, Author, and Speaker with a passion for helping others learn to be at Peace and rise to their fullest potential.

He is the developer of *The Language of Ho'oponopono,* a process that takes ho'oponopono to the deepest levels of self-forgiveness to bring body, mind, and spirit into harmony.

Jon weaves quantum physics, metaphysics, religion, neuroplasticity, and simple common sense into a blanket of easy-to-understand tools that make it simple to practice complex principles, guiding us to the evolution of the person we are meant to be.

Jon Lovgren
Website: http://themagicwords.net/

Facebook:
https://www.facebook.com/JustSayThem

Email: jon@themagicwords.net

Printed in Great Britain
by Amazon